Your Dreams
and Your Stars

Your Dreams and Your Stars

David F. Melbourne and Helen Adams

BLANDFORD

A BLANDFORD BOOK

First published in the UK 1998 by Blandford
A Cassell imprint

Cassell plc
Wellington House
125 Strand
London WC2R OBB

Distributed in the United States by Sterling Publishing Co. Inc.,
387 Park Avenue South, New York, NY 10016-8810

A Cataloguing-in-Publication Data entry for this title
is available from the British Library

ISBN 0-7137-2689-X

Printed and bound in Great Britain
by MPG Books Limited, Bodmin, Cornwall

*

*To Elizabeth,
who is courageously coping
with multiple sclerosis.*

*

Contents

Foreword

iterally anything is possible, according to the new concepts about our existence and environment that are gradually replacing the limited, physically-based 'Science' which most of us were taught at school. Even orthodox science must now consider sub-atomic particles that can be in two places at once. Science has been less than impartial in not accepting the paranormal anomalies of existence that ordinary people know happen, yet which scientists would not countenance because their theories have obscured the facts. Certainly, the notion that everything was near to being explained once and for all by science now appears pompous and risible.

My own contribution to the long-due overthrow of conventional thinking in science is to restate and develop the concept that we exist in a mentalistic rather than a physical universe. That view, which emerged naturally from my studies of lucid dreaming and, in particular, premonitions, opens a new and limitless vista on what can happen in our experience. It embraces all the 'unacceptable' phenomena which narrow-minded science has ignored for so long: telepathy, clairvoyance, precognition, astrology, miracles, past lives and synchronicities, for example. In this scheme of things, the macrocosm and microcosm ('As above, so below') are closely related, as the ancients wisely observed.

We were all brought up to develop a particular mind-set in our perception of the universe and our understanding of it. Those of us who seek the real truth have had to throw off that straitjacket of conditioning and look at things from a wider viewpoint. Thus, in astrology, to consider critically the minuscule gravitational attraction of distant planets is the wrong approach. What is more important is simply the planets' existence in our shared consciousness. If something exists (a planet or the memory of a dead person, say), it can exert an effect – no matter how far it is away in time or space. It is clear that everything is interrelated. From this new position, astrology can be seen to hold a perfectly valid place in our lives.

Astrology has a long history of careful observation and refinement, which should be respected. Even in conventional science, strong links between birth date and choice of profession have been noted. As he describes in *The Cosmic Clocks* (Paladin, 1973), Gauquelin found definite correlations between these factors and posited the operation of a sort of cosmic biology.

During my own researches, I have uncovered an association between the birth dates of psychic people and the lunar cycle. More psychics are born at the time of the full moon and new moon than at other times in the cycle, and psychics tend to be born in the winter months (November to February), with a sharp decline in the birth dates of these people in October. I feel that there are many important phenomena waiting to be discovered by scientists who are bold enough to investigate this fascinating area.

Dream analysis, too, has advanced considerably in recent decades. The limitations of adopting a specific, rigid framework (such as the Freudian version) have been recognized, and sensible methods are now employed by many interpreters. My own work has discovered various consistent effects in dreams (the light-switch phenomenon, for instance) that are the result of limitations in the dream-producing process and are not directly symbolic. A recent advance in interpretation has been the introduction of the flow-chart system, developed by David Melbourne.

A synthesis of dream interpretation and astrology – the topic of this book – is a natural progression to an understanding of ourselves. It might be termed 'astro-oneiroscopy'. To put it simply, with David's technique, the individual's basic astrological imprint at birth and other chart information are used to reveal extra valuable insights into the meaning of their dreams. I welcome the development and look forward to seeing the results of this powerful dual approach.

Dr Keith Hearne
Hurst, Berkshire, 1996

Acknowledgements

The authors would like to thank Joan Newby, for checking the manuscript and making some excellent suggestions, and everybody who, over the years, has sent in dreams for analysis; this book would not have been possible without them.

Introduction

iving on the remote island of Hoy in the archipelago of Orkney has its advantages. The serenity of island life allows us to focus our thoughts and, if we desire, to get in touch with the inner self. Orkney seems to attract people from towns and cities who are tired of the rat race and want to explore spirituality and mysticism.

I first became interested in dream interpretation after I underwent my second near-death experience, or NDE. The powerful spirituality of the event, which occurred during my service with the London Fire Brigade, changed my life for ever, by starting me on a psychic quest.

Time seemed to stand still, while, trapped on a burning roof, I witnessed a review of my life. Although the incident lasted only a few moments, it was as if I had unlimited time to ponder each scene as it appeared in my mind's eye.

My conscious self did not part company from my body, as it had during my first NDE, which happened at the age of three, when I came close to drowning. Nevertheless, the experience was so profound that I knew without a doubt that I possessed an immortal soul. In addition, every year since my escape from the fire, I have had at least two out of body experiences.

After that fateful event, I became increasingly eager for knowledge of the metaphysical. During my studies, I focused on the idea that we might all share a collective consciousness. The more I thought about this, the more sense it seemed to make.

The notion that we all share a consciousness on a subconscious level, which might contain boundless wisdom and knowledge, led me to consider ways of accessing it. I became interested in dreams. Many inventions, cures for diseases, works of art, great literature and other outstanding discoveries have been inspired or directly gleaned from dreams. Therefore, it seemed reasonable to me that dreams might also be alerting us to other aspects of our lives.

First, I began to interpret dreams for my wife and one or two close friends. After studying Freud, Jung, the Gestalt theory and other approaches to dream interpretation, I started to develop my own method of analysis. It soon transpired that I was achieving a high level of accuracy. However, when I got it wrong, I did so in spectacular fashion.

During my researches, I came across the writings of Dr Keith Hearne, the author of the foreword of this book. Over the years, this brilliant scientist had been running sleep laboratories. He was studying lucid dreams (in which dreamers become fully cognizant of the fact that they are dreaming, and may control the dream), and was the first person to establish structured communication between a dreaming subject and the outside world.

Although research into lucid dreaming is still in its infancy and has far to go, there is little doubt that it has enormous potential; skilled conscious manipulation of a dream can give access to almost limitless knowledge.

Dr Hearne also discovered other factors in dreams which were to lead me to crack the code of dream interpretation, thus eliminating further spectacular failures.

Then came the opportunity to put my theory to the test: I interpreted a dream for Dr Hearne. He was sufficiently impressed to want to find out about my methodology. Ultimately, our association led to our collaboration in writing *Dream Interpretation – The Secret* (Blandford Press, 1997). (For readers who wish to achieve a high level of accuracy in dream analysis, it would be advisable to begin by studying this book, as it discusses in detail my flow-chart method of dream interpretation, which can only be briefly outlined here.)

I currently produce a two-page column on the subject of dreams for *Horoscope* magazine, for which I also regularly supply short stories drawn from my own creative dreams. Through my connection with the magazine, I have naturally become more and more interested in the subject of astrology.

For example, I have begun to carry out research designed to discover whether the pull of the moon affects our dreams. If I can isolate a common theme in vivid dreams that occur during the phase of the new moon or the full moon, it would support the theory of astrological influence on human affairs. If the moon can affect our dreams, so might other heavenly bodies. And if they can affect our dreams, then why not our behaviour and personality too?

Helen Adams, the co-author of this book, was one of those who decided to move to the island of Hoy so that she could pursue her shamanic and astrological studies in tranquil surroundings. Helen speedily became known in Orkney for her accurate charts and forecasts. Particularly evident was her talent for extraordinarily accurate astrological psychological profiles.

During one of my daily outings to the local post office, I met Helen and we began to discuss astrology and dream interpretation. It didn't take long to realize that we share similar interests, and became friends.

Some time later, Helen had a vivid dream which intrigued her. When I interepreted it, the message that emerged was closely allied to her interest in shamanism. In turn, Helen did an astrological forecast for the year ahead for me, which turned out to be stunningly accurate.

Then, one day, we were speculating as to whether dreams and their interpretation might have any links with astrology. After all, astrology has been connected to just about everything else: diet, health, love, sex and money, for example. I gave Helen a client's dream to work on. 'See what you come up with,' I said.

We were amazed when her astrological profile paralleled my interpretation. Almost exactly the same features were uncovered.

After close comparison, we found the results were uncannily alike, apart from a difference at the end of the interpretation. Even that disparity proved to be a variation on the same theme – the other side of the same coin, so to speak.

The flow-chart method concentrates on the dream itself, whereas the astrological interpretation addresses the subject's psyche (conscious and unconscious), and the character traits deduced from their birth chart. Therefore, each interpretation deals with different aspects of the dream and the dreamer. Nevertheless, there are invariably points where both methods come together. It is on these aspects that the analyst should concentrate most attention.

Through a process of natural progression, we discovered that if the flow-chart analysis and the astrological analysis are first read separately, and then together, the points at which they overlap or meet highlight aspects of the dream's deeper message. In other words, this approach provides an holistic interpretation which homes in on the heart of the dream's message, and it generally offers valuable advice as to how the dreamer might improve their quality of life.

Since those early days, we have found, to our delight, that this in-depth, holistic method of dream analysis provides new insights into the dreamer's life and can bring hitherto inaccessible and potentially life-enhancing benefits.

We thus discovered a definite link between dream interpretation and astrology. We were so excited by our findings that, by way of a commemoration, the first dream studied in this book (see Chapter 1) is the one we first analysed in tandem.

In effect, the fact that both methods identify similar (sometimes startlingly similar) themes constitutes evidence which seems to support the validity of both dream interpretation and astrology. The unbiased comments from our subjects about the interpretations of their dreams indicate that they are convinced of its accuracy. Who better to judge?

I have no doubt that this combined technique is a method of dream interpretation which far exceeds what would normally be expected from an analyst. Our interpretations do much more than decode the message concealed in a dream. They suggest ways in which the dreamer can act on that message in order to harmonize discordant factors in their lives.

Let us hope that this is just the beginning. Perhaps other like-minded analysts and astrologers will further develop our findings. Who knows what revelations might come to light?

David Melbourne
Orkney

ver since I can remember, I have been fascinated by the unexplained and the mysterious. Given a choice, I would have no hesitation in choosing a book of folk-tales, myths and legends, even one without pictures, over any other plaything. My imagination would transport me to strange realms in times before time where dragons lived, wizards walked and heroes performed feats of great courage and chivalry.

Having 'grown up', I have found that my childhood instincts were unerringly accurate in guiding me towards what has become the main focus of my life. I have always been interested in what lies behind the known and the obvious, the invisible hand that causes the sun to rise and set, the moon to wax and wane, the revolving cycle of the seasons and the many moods and natures of people around the world.

So it is really no surprise that I have long been drawn towards the subject of astrology, in which I became seriously involved about fifteen years ago. Wishing to learn more of the subject, I enrolled with a certain astrological institution, only to find their methods somewhat limited and not particularly inspiring. I then discovered a course run by Howard Sasportas, who has since passed away. His approach was both inspiring and dynamic, focusing on the underlying mythology of the various signs and planets. Under his tuition the whole birth chart came alive for me, and what had previously seemed like a set of symbols became imbued with life and energy.

As well as learning with Howard Sasportas, I also regularly attended lectures by Liz Greene, and found these equally inspiring, as they tied together the contents of the chart with different psychological patterns and archetypes. Astrology became a dynamic tool for focusing on inner psychological processes, and for helping people to find meaning and a reason for events in their lives which may previously have caused confusion and pain.

From these beginnings I began to interpret birth charts for friends and family, to read books constantly and to further and update my knowledge.

Over the past eight years or so I have been practising astrology on a professional basis, using my knowledge of the inner psychological workings of the mind and blending the approaches of such people as Carl Jung and Roberto Assagioli, who developed the process of psychosynthesis.

I see astrology as a language of energy which reveals the cyclical process by which change can be forecast and understood, and which accurately describes not only the way a given person's various energies interact, but the unique view that they have of the world. It shows the context in which a person is experiencing both inner symbols and outer events. In other words, it applies to both the inner and the outer circumstances of each human being. While this may be a simplification, it suggests the profound potential of astrology for understanding and interpreting the complex array of human experience.

In 1989 I moved from London up to Scotland, and a couple of years later up to the Island of Hoy, as my partner and I had always been attracted by the extraordinary beauty of the place and the way of life there, which brought us closer to nature.

I now divide my time between astrological work, which includes natal interpretations, future trends, particular personal problems, relationship and composite charts, and writing and teaching. However, one of my main interests is resolving the dilemmas which are clearly revealed on the birth chart and introducing a healing element.

As an astrologer, I often have the task of explaining to clients why certain areas of their lives are not working as they would wish; they may be faced with a difficult decision which only they can make. It is as though the source of the problem has been located and now what they need is to go further to resolve the issue in question.

One particular method of dealing with such problems is described in *The Inner Guide Meditation* by Edwin C. Steinbrecher. Steinbrecher has developed a way of finding one's inner guide and combining the imagery of tarot and the natal chart to work on inner realms and resolve the blocks and challenges outlined in the astrological chart. Many of his subjects have experienced dramatic changes in their lives, especially in the situations which were the source of their troubles. However, although this method has been very successful, it did not seem quite right for me.

I then became very interested in the shamanic path, a method of gaining help and guidance which has been used virtually since the dawn of time. The shamanic way understands that the whole of life, both the physical and non-physical dimensions, are interrelated; everything is connected to everything else in a kind of cosmic web. Within this web there are three worlds: the lower world, which relates to our ancestors and the roots of things; the middle world, which is concerned with our everyday life and practical affairs, and includes the physical dimension of the earth; and the upper world, the one which perhaps pertains most to astrology and the natal chart, because it relates to the 'blueprint' of things, the bigger picture. The upper world is a realm of potential, of vision and of what could be. Here we can tune into our own highest destiny and obtain guidance to rediscover our path when we have lost our connection.

A gentle drum-beat in the background facilitates journeys to these other dimensions, the drumming helping to cut out interference from the conscious mind. I personally have obtained invaluable guidance and help using the shamanic method. I am currently experimenting to see whether parallels can be drawn between the natal chart and the experiences in these inner depths and, if so, how these can be used to help clients resolve their dilemmas.

My meeting with David Melbourne and his wife Chris opened up a whole new dimension in accessing these inner realms. David has refined his method of dream interpretation to a high level of accuracy and has had a lot of success in decoding the most difficult and enigmatic of dreams. His reputation is fast spreading, not only in this country, but world-wide.

So it was perhaps a happy coincidence that we came up with the idea of experimenting with combining astrology and dream interpretation, as this provides an immediate way of accessing the inner worlds in order to release the guiding function of the higher self.

Using the natal chart as the background for the interpretation seems to put the dream into a broader context. The natal chart is divided into twelve sections, each relating to a different area of our lives, and it is possible, by connecting the symbolism of the dream to the natal chart, to identify the area of life with which the dream is concerned.

Furthermore, different dream characters seem to relate to the action of certain planets in their relationship to sign, house and aspects to other planets. This sheds more light on the interpretation and reveals more about the inner dynamics of the dream.

Another interesting factor to consider is that of transits, the movement of the planets in relation to the chart itself. Sometimes it is difficult to tell whether a forthcoming connection between two planets will result in an outer event, an inner realization, or in both. By noting the time of clients' dreams, however, it can be seen that certain dreams tie in with transits, as if to reinforce the inner messages that the subconscious self is trying to relay to the conscious mind.

This brings us to another intriguing subject: signs and omens. If we decode the meaning of a dream message at a relatively early stage, we can take steps to avert potential untoward events in our lives, and there will be no need for the message to be communicated more urgently. If we do not, our subconscious or inner wisdom will try to get our attention by creating signs, or ominous events, in the environment around us. If we ignore or do not notice these, a significant external event will materialize and we shall be forced to deal with its consequences. Using the birth chart and the dream together can make us aware of such signs early on, so that we can take action before the situation becomes too serious.

David and I both feel that combining the information in the natal chart with the dream and its analysis offers another dimension to dream interpretation. We all sometimes wonder why certain events are happening in our lives; we pray for inspiration and answers to our problems. The combination of dream analysis and astrolgical interpretation amplifies the beneficial effects of the dream function, one of the most common ways of receiving guidance since time began.

We hope that the continued application of this method will be the catalyst for many new ways of healing the lives of individuals and even, on a wider scale, our planet.

Helen Adams
Orkney

CHAPTER 1

Sue's Dream

he descriptions of individual dreams included in this book will be accompanied by explanations of our methods of analysis. A brief evaluation of our findings follows each dream appraisal. For those unfamiliar with astrology, we recommend Elaine Smith's *Astrology – The Inner Eye* (see Recommended Reading). Readers may also find the Appendix (page 181) and Glossary (page 184) useful.

In order to demonstrate the amazing potential of this new system of holistic interpretation, we are starting with the original dream which eventually led to the writing of this book.

Sue, our first subject, told us that, during the sixties, she was a great fan of George Harrison, one of the four famous Beatles. She was a single parent until her son reached the age of eight.

SUBJECT:
* Sue W.
* British
* Born 11.25 am, 15 August 1947
* Chiropodist
* Divorced, with one son
* Introvert, but projects extrovert image

The Dream

* *I am in a queue for something, maybe a show or a concert, exactly what is unclear. We're not queuing on foot, however, but in a large vehicle, something like a coach. I'm an onlooker with no physical form. Yet I know that the George Harrison figure in this queue is supposed to be me. My son is with me as a little boy, so we're in the late-sixties period.*

My son goes missing and I find him in a building familiar to me. I think it's the day nursery he used to go to while I was at work.

The staff are holding me to ransom and demanding money for his return. I (as George Harrison) am very assertive and promise to sue them for every penny they have if they do any harm to him. Eventually, they let me have him for £7.50. ✳

Flow-chart Interpretation

This dream was very interesting and revealing, but most of all, admirable. It is evident that Sue is a very good mum – her son certainly didn't go short of her love when he was younger. We also gather from the dream that they are still close. Moreover, it tells us that she is a lady of high principles. Although she still has a yearning for some excitement at times, she won't allow it to come in the way of her responsibilities or her career.

The dream begins with a queue. People queue either for something they need, as in the days of rationing, or, as in this case, for something they want to see or experience. Although the reason is unclear, Sue mentions a show or concert. So we have a situation which points to anticipated excitement.

However, this wasn't the overriding factor. The fact that she doesn't know whether she is waiting to see a concert indicates that it is not as important as it would once have been.

She is queuing in a coach (somewhat detached). This supports the interpretation so far, in that she is not taking an active part in a physical, pushing and shoving queue.

She has no form, so we are definitely dealing with her subconscious. This is confirmed when she sees a 'George Harrison figure' who is supposed to be her. George represents somebody she liked, but also somebody she admired. Therefore, in this instance, her subconscious is drawing our attention to the masculine side of her character – her assertiveness, perhaps. (We all have a shadow, or opposite, side.)

Next, her son is with her (as a little boy). This immediately tells us that we are dealing with the part of her that sometimes yearns for the excitement and feelings of past years, which everyone craves from time to time. The dream has alerted us to character traits Sue used to have.

The scene is set: we are dealing with a part of her character which is still somewhat wayward, the part which looks for romance (George), excitement (the concert) and the freedom to let her hair down occasionally.

The son serves two purposes in this dream. First, to indicate a specific period in Sue's life, thereby telling us which part of her character the dream is dealing with. Second, he acts as the pivot to the entire message of the dream. The fact that he goes missing symbolizes that those days have gone.

It is crucial, in order to achieve an accurate dream interpretation, to know a few facts about the dreamer. Often, as in this case, the analyst must pay close attention to any background information the subject provides in addition to the description of the dream itself. Sue's remarks proved extremely helpful. In this context, it is clear that, like most people, she misses a past time of excitement (the sixties) when she was able, to a certain extent, to be happy-go-lucky.

However, knowing that she had her son at the tender age of nineteen helped to steer us through the analysis. She didn't have the opportunity to be irresponsible. She missed a few years when her peers would have been partying and so forth. Instead, she elected to be a responsible and loving mother (in the dream, she was enraged when her son went missing).

Now we come to the crux of the dream: Sue's son was taken to the day nursery (a place where he was looked after while she went to work). This clearly represents a dependable attitude towards work and responsibilities. In the form of George, she was assertive and threatened to sue (her own name) for every penny (meaning she would give her all). Eventually, she got him back for £7.50, which was a tidy sum in the sixties, possibly equivalent to a week's wages.

There is clearly a side to Sue's character which likes to live the exciting life, perhaps including parties, music, booze and all the things she missed out on when she was younger, but she is now evolving beyond that. Although she would still enjoy letting her hair down occasionally, it isn't as important to her as it used to be. Now she is protecting her way of life – job, career, hobbies, etc. (as indicated by the nursery in the dream) – instead of her son, whom she had to protect before.

Therefore, the dream is showing that she won't let enjoyment side-track her if it would be detrimental to what she values. In other words, her subconscious is reinforcing the inner strength she has and helping her to resist certain things, and live without them, for as long as necessary. Those lost days are not as significant as they used be.

We learnt a lot from this dream. Sue enjoys a good laugh and can be quite outgoing when it suits her, perhaps even have the devil in her at times, but she is sorting out her priorities. She is fulfilling her potential and evolving into a whole person: someone who knows what her priorities are and where she is going and is willing to make sacrifices to get there (the £7:50). She has acknowledged that, although there can still be exciting times, they are no longer as important as they used to be. In other words, it would appear that she is getting her life in order and is firmly in charge of her own destiny.

The message behind the dream does not paint Sue as a happy-go-lucky person, nor one who is in any way irresponsible. It is merely pointing to one facet of her personality and letting her know that she is in control of that part of her life. It is a dream which offers comfort and reassurance.

* * *

The dream interpretation which we offered was confirmed as accurate by the subject, who commented: 'I was thrilled when I saw the interpretation. You have helped me to understand and make sense of it.'

Now let us take a look at the same dream from the astrological viewpoint to see what conclusions we reach.

Astrological Interpretation

The symbolism in Sue's natal chart bore quite an accurate resemblance to that in her dream.

Sue has a Libra ascendant, which means that at first she comes across as being friendly and sociable, wanting to make a good impression, and possibly quite anxious to please. However, this image is quickly dispelled by the presence of six planets (Sun, Moon, Mercury, Venus, Saturn and Pluto) in Leo in the section of her chart related to authority, career issues, father, public image and responsibility. This means that Sue rates her career very highly, striving to be an authority herself, and that to have a place of standing in the community is very important to her.

Having so many planets in such a positive masculine sign as Leo shows that Sue likes to be the centre of attention, and dislikes taking second place. Leos have an inherently royal nature and feel that they were born to rule wherever life places them. Sue would not take any form of criticism very well and at times she may appear forceful and overbearing, determined to have her own way at all costs.

The natal chart usually affords many clues as to how we can maintain a state of balance in our lives, and in this instance there are several. First, Neptune situated in Libra, in the section of the chart related to spirituality, mysticism and the unconscious mind, shows that Sue has a strong spiritual element in her nature. Neptune is the planet of inspiration and a kind of refined state of consciousness. It is also the planet of illusion and confusion and its placement reveals that Sue's spiritual nature is functioning underground; it has not yet fully come into her awareness, although it is most definitely there.

Neptune in Libra also shows that it is important for her to reach a state of balance between the inner and outer expressions of her nature, to be able to recognize her spiritual side and harmonize this with her outer persona.

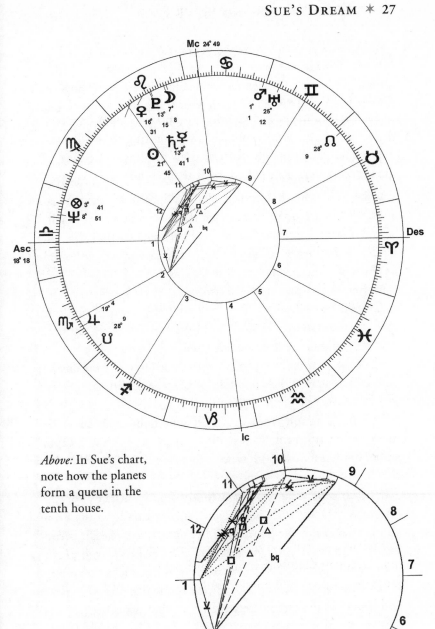

Above: In Sue's chart, note how the planets form a queue in the tenth house.

Right: Enlarged detail of central circle.

Another clue is the presence of what is known as the North Node (a point in the chart which shows what we need to work on during our lives) in the section of her chart related to change and transformation. This is linked to such transitions as birth, marriage, death or the end of one way of life and the beginning of a new one as the result of a change in thinking.

The presence of the North Node here suggests that Sue would benefit from looking beyond appearances to the underlying reality of a person, situation or relationship. She would then gain a deeper understanding of her own motives and those of others.

The North Node is in Taurus, which suggests that she has a tendency to take things too literally at times, or even to impose her own blocks in order not to see.

Jupiter in Scorpio, in the section of the chart related to personal finances and possessions and issues of self-worth, indicates that she may uncover something of great value, inner resources which she did not realize she possessed.

If Sue can balance the spiritual with the material, many areas of her experience would tend to take on a deeper meaning, reflected in a more satisfying and happy life.

This information from the chart may help us discover the meaning of her dream. We will also look at the astrological transits and progressions which were in force around the time she had the dream, to see if these reveal any clues.

In her dream, Sue is in a queue for something, maybe a show or a concert, exactly what is unclear. This waiting for a big event strongly relates to the Leo side of her nature, as this sign is connected with entertainment and also with celebrities and people with great charisma. The fact that she is in a queue is interesting, because that is precisely the condition of the planets in her tenth and eleventh house: they are actually in a line or queue.

What we need to find out is which sides of her nature (represented by the planets) she has adopted in the queue. The clue comes from her words 'in a large vehicle, something like a coach'. The planet Mercury is related to movement, travel and vehicles, so one of the characters is represented by the principle of travel, movement, communication and the exchange of information.

She also says, 'I'm an onlooker, with no physical form. Yet I know that the George Harrison figure in this queue is supposed to be me.' This figure relates to her Sun in Leo. The Sun represents the self and also the centre of the self. The formation of a strong inner foundation, often discussed by psychologists such as Carl Jung, is a lifetime's work.

Sue says that in the dream she has no physical form, which could indicate a level of consciousness she is working towards. It is probably something which is in the process of coming into being; something she aspires to, but has not yet attained. We also feel that her son, as a child, represents another aspect of the Sun. Here we have the higher self shown as George Harrison and the child, her son, symbolizing a spontaneous and fun-loving aspect of the self.

There are two principles at work: communication and state of being. These two principles set the scene. The fact that both are situated in the section of the chart connected with authority, career and issues shows that this is the background situation to which the dream refers.

Sue describes how her son goes missing and she finds him in a building similar to a day nursery in which he used to stay when she was at work. This could refer to an aspect of her being, her inner child, which has gone missing. Could this mean that her inner child has been relegated to another place in her psyche, while she concentrates on work issues?

The staff are holding her son to ransom and demanding money for his return. In Sue's chart, staff or employees are represented in the sixth house by Pisces, which is ruled by the planet Neptune. Neptune is actually situated in the area of the chart related to the unconscious mind, spirituality and past karma. As mentioned above, Neptune also refers to Sue's own latent spirituality. Perhaps the staff represent the unconscious mind, which is difficult to access; this could be why there is a price to pay for his return.

Sue is obviously very angry at discovering the loss and states that, as George Harrison, she is very assertive, threatening to 'sue them for every penny they have if they do any harm to him'. As we have seen, George Harrison represents the spiritually aware and conscious side of her self, which feels enraged at losing the child to the hidden depths of the subconscious realms. Something very precious to Sue has been allowed to slip back into unawareness. The Sun, as a centre of integration and balance, recognizes a need for wholeness, for being all that one is, rather than fragmented.

This is also where the principle of movement and communication, as represented by Mercury, comes into play. Sue has had to barter vigorously, to make a deal with the staff, in order to retrieve her son unharmed. It would seem that communication with these inner elements of her own nature will be the turning-point in recovering the child.

We feel that part of the message in the astrological reading is that Sue needs to turn within and begin to develop the spiritual and childlike qualities of spontaneity and a non-judgemental outlook, but that there is a price to pay. In the dream, she duly pays this price and the child is returned to her. Perhaps the sum of £7.50 represents not just money but Sue's age: at seven, some event may have happened for which she feels she paid a heavy price, and she may now have reached a turning-point in resolving that event.

This idea is borne out by the symbolism associated with money in her chart. Personal finances, possessions and issues of self-worth are under the sign of Scorpio, which in turn is ruled by Pluto. Pluto is placed in Leo and is part of the group of six planets. It deals with past issues, where we hold on to energy patterns which are no longer relevant to our current situation. In this case, Pluto specifically refers to parental issues, especially concerning the father. When the old patterns are re-examined and the energy released, the person is free to adopt new and more constructive behaviour patterns.

Self-esteem appears to be a strong factor in this dream – a price was actually mentioned – and the fact that the George Harrison figure was assertive and got what he wanted shows that Sue has the capacity to make the required changes in her life.

If we look at the transits and progressions around the time of the dream, it is clear that Sue is standing at a threshold. Over the coming years, certain factors in her chart will be initiating a kind of opening-up and developing process. Pluto, which has now moved into Sagittarius, will be making harmonious aspects to the line of six planets in Leo. This heralds a time of widening experience, when she will learn to use the various energies in a positive way. There may be changes and many death-and-rebirth scenarios, but it is likely that she will become more open to change as time goes on.

Uranus has also moved into its own sign of Aquarius and will make challenging aspects to the same six planets over the next few years. Sue will begin to see many of her former behaviour patterns in a new light and from a different perspective. In the year of this dream, Sue's progressed Moon moves into the section of her chart related to change and transformation. She will have to contend with issues which involve the end of one way of life and the beginning of a new one.

It seems that she is on the verge of making changes to her thinking and behaviour, and that she is getting her priorities right.

Summary

Although there are differences between them, both analyses deal with the same central aspects of Sue's situation. She has decided to put the exciting times behind her in order to concentrate on her work and career and – this is a vital point – she is acting responsibly in performing her duties.

In addition, her chart reveals that she tends to concentrate on work issues to the detriment of other, equally important, areas of her life. Using her chart to aid interpretation of the dream symbols reveals that an essential component of her psychic wholeness has slipped back into her unconscious. Her higher self believes its retrieval is necessary if she is to live more fully. We feel that the dream is also suggesting that she take the next step in her development by consciously cultivating open-mindedness, spontaneity, acceptance and the ability to move with the flow of life rather than against it.

* * *

When Sue, the subject of this dream, saw the interpretation, she commented:

> I find the concept of a tie-up between astrology and dreams fascinating. There certainly does seem to be a link, as there were such striking similarities between the two interpretations, even though they had been arrived at quite differently.
>
> While two seemingly different conclusions were drawn, they are both correct. I can see the sense and logic of each method and will take all the good advice on board and act on it. I have put everything on hold to further my career, but now that I am achieving a measure of success, maybe I can once again make time for myself and take up some of the hobbies and interests I used to enjoy. It's going to be a little more difficult for me to awaken the spiritual side of my nature, but I'm sure that once I can achieve a better balance in life, I shall be all the richer for it.

Comparisons and Conclusions

The two approaches to dream interpretation revealed different, but highly important, information about Sue, and both enhanced her understanding of herself.

As we pointed out in the Introduction, the flow-chart system deals directly with the dream, whereas the astrological analysis concentrates mainly on individual aspects of the dreamer's psychology, and it is on the areas where both analyses meet that the client's attention should be concentrated: these are the issues at the heart of the dream.

In this sense, both analyses point to a period of change in Sue's life, a time for sorting out her priorities. Each homes in on issues of her career, her child and her social life. However, as one would expect, the astrological reading unearths more layers of Sue's personality, and does so in astonishing detail.

The first interpretation reassures Sue about her conscious role in society. She has responsibilities to which she must attend and therefore cannot allow herself to be side-tracked. She is reorganizing her life and has certain goals and ambitions which she must reach in order to succeed.

Using the natal chart to consider other aspects of the dream, it is evident that Sue would be mistaken to see her work and career as the be-all and end-all of her life. However, her work is important to her because it enables her to contribute positively to society and this role is an essential part of her nature. To deny this would be to deny her *raison d'être*.

Nevertheless, certain other aspects of her psyche need to be brought into balance. In this dream her attention is being drawn to the natural, spontaneous and childlike side of her personality, which she has pushed away, possibly seeing it as having no real value in her current situation, although both the George Harrison figure and the staff in her dream realize its worth.

Some months after Sue received her holistic analysis, we contacted her again to find out whether she had acted on the advice given. We were delighted to discover that she was now a much happier person.

Having studied both analyses together in some depth, Sue had recognized that her left brain was far too dominant in her life – she wasn't making enough time for herself. She came to this realization after taking up meditation, which has taught her how to balance the different aspects dealt with by each hemisphere of the brain more efficiently. Now she makes sure that there is space in her diary just for her. Apart from meditation, she sets aside much more time to pursue her hobby of painting and to listen to music.

This has apparently had a beneficial effect on her life. She feels much more relaxed and in control; she doesn't worry as much, and she is far less uptight than she used to be.

Sue explained that the analysis had made her realize that her work was dominating her life. This understanding made her take stock and introduce some changes. Already, she has achieved a much better balance in her life.

What about her doubts about cultivating her spiritual side? She told us that developing a better balance by allowing more right-brain activities seemed to lead naturally to a more spiritual approach to everyday life.

By acting on the issues highlighted by the holistic interpretation, Sue has reaped substantial rewards. As a result, she no longer feels under the amount of pressure that the pursuit of her career had previously caused. Her stress levels have been reduced substantially, and she has learned to relax and enjoy pastimes of a creative nature. This in turn has enhanced her spirituality.

The holistic technique of dream analysis has clearly had a healing effect on Sue's mind, body and spirit. She has learned to relax (mind); the risk of stress-related diseases has been reduced (body), and she feels more in touch with her inner self (spirit).

Moreover, there seems to be another valuable advantage which, so far, has been ignored. Perhaps the most striking thing is that Sue reported that her work has not suffered at all; on the contrary, it seems to be running as efficiently as ever – perhaps more so. This seems paradoxical, considering that the dream message she received was to concentrate less on her work and make more time for herself. Perhaps another paradox provides the answer: the more haste, the less speed!

CHAPTER 2

Dream Symbols

s the variation between different schools of thought regarding analysis and dream symbols is the biggest single reason for inaccuracy in dream interpretation, we will begin by examining these issues in the light of David's hypotheses, arrived at after more than 20 years of painstaking reasearch.

That Freud made valuable contributions to dream interpretation cannot be denied; it is evident the purpose of many dreams is indeed wish-fulfilment, as he maintained. Jung added many important hypotheses, perhaps the greatest of which was the existence of a collective consciousness to which we all have access. Perls' Gestalt theory also provides useful insights and can help solve puzzling dreams. For instance, by stretching this theory, David realized that dream images of the right and left side, or male and female, can be references to the right and left hemispheres of the brain. Others, including Ullman, Faraday and Adler, put forward valid theories, and the dream beliefs of ancient cultures are worth serious consideration, too.

It would be a mistake to assert that only Freud or Jung, for instance, was right, although that is precisely what many analysts seem to do. Followers of Jung are often at odds with students of Freud – but why? It is more reasonable to assume that no one person could have found all the answers. It makes sense to accept that all theories have a contribution to make in such an indubitably vast field as dream interpretation.

It can take many years of hard work before a dream analyst feels reasonably confident that he or she can make an accurate interpretation, and it is only by checking the results with the subject that any theory can be put to the test. Analysts must constantly seek feedback from their clients in order to monitor the level of accuracy they are achieving.

In a single dream, David has identified features relating to Freud's wish-fulfilment hypothesis, Jung's idea about collective consciousness, and Gestalt theory. This highlights the necessity to learn as much as possible from all schools of thought and the futility of following only one.

Unfortunately, many would-be dream analysts, with little thought, adopt a dangerously blinkered approach. They often settle for their favourite dream dictionary and argue that its definition of dream images and symbols is the only correct one.

Such dictionary definitions cannot be relied upon. The authors assert that the interpretations are valid because they have been passed down the centuries, but no evidence founded on concrete research exists to justify these claims. (How, for example, do they arrive at definitions of symbols relating to modern-day machinery?) The fact that dream dictionaries generally disagree with each other must surely cast grave doubts on their credibility.

To illustrate how they can be dangerous, one dream dictionary states that to dream of walking on somebody else's grave means that death is imminent. Such an interpretation is outrageous and irresponsible, without basis in fact, and is certainly not the product of diligent research.

Imagine that the person consulting the dictionary for an interpretation of such a dream suffers from severe depression and has a sweetheart who is seriously ill. Their depression might worsen to a point where they decide to commit suicide – a worst-case scenario, but a feasible one.

We concede the possibility that universal symbols may exist. However, David has yet to find a symbol that means the same for every dreamer. To say that a dream about a phoenix, for example, represents a new beginning from the ashes of despair (the universal symbolic meaning) might turn out to be accurate. However, after putting all the necessary questions, one might learn that the subject comes from Phoenix, Arizona, or is a fire-fighter, or looks after birds which have been rescued. What conclusion would be reached if it came to light that the subject was a student of myth and legend?

There are far too many variables to consider when assessing symbolic meanings: the subject's nationality, age, sex, occupation, temperament and so on. Other factors to be explored include the action, dialogue, setting and emotion of the dream. What part did the symbol play in the dream (if any) and how did it tie in with the general contents of the dream?

Suppose one dreamed of a herd of cattle, for instance; what would it mean? Dream dictionaries suggest a host of nonsensical and groundless meanings, from good fortune to financial loss or even disgrace. To find the true meaning, one must address many questions and seek information about the dreamer.

For example, the dreamer may come from Argentina and have a family history of cattle farming, or from India, where cattle are held to be sacred. An office worker in London, less obviously, may associate cattle with the sanctuary of his or her country cottage. If the subject is a sailor from Kent, the old superstition held by Kentish seamen that it is unlucky to have cattle on board a ship might provide a clue.

The dream analyst must delve far deeper to establish the real meaning. In what sort of setting did the cattle appear? Were they standing calmly, stampeding, grazing, lying down? What part did the dreamer play (if any)? Was the dream accompanied by emotion? If so, what kind, and why? Was there any dialogue, and did it relate to the cattle? Were other symbols involved? Were they associated with the cattle?

Taking these questions into account, it is evident that there is almost no limit to the meanings which could be attributed to a dream about cattle. But it doesn't end there. Invariably, there will be other factors in the dream which will have to be investigated, including other symbols, people, settings and dialogue.

Accurate dream interpretation takes hours of hard investigative work; there is no magic solution that one can simply pluck out of the air. No one would consider it reasonable to go to a doctor, complaining of feeling unwell, then expect him or her to make a diagnosis without asking questions about their symptoms or performing an examination. Yet that is precisely what some people expect when seeking a dream interpretation. 'Come on then, tell me what it means,' is often the challenge.

Nowadays, if we are requested to give an instant interpretation, we generally refuse. In the past, we have made such attempts, only to discover later that we were completely wrong. For the reader who has ever been furnished with such an interpretation, we urge caution.

Recently, David received a letter from an Asian gentleman who, years ago, paid to have a dream interpreted. The fraudulent lady who claimed to be an analyst gave an instant reading which warned this poor man that he was in for a bumpy ride and that his luck would be bad. Since then, nothing seemed to have gone right for him. He listed a catalogue of disasters which included the loss of a business, a failed career and a broken marriage. When we studied this man's dream, however, we were unable to find anything in it to warrant such an alarming interpretation.

Because he had been brought up in a culture which sets great store in oracular systems, he was predisposed to believe the prediction. Consequently, there is every reason to suspect that his run of bad luck was the result of a self-fulfiling prophesy. In other words, it is more than likely that, being so convinced by the interpretation, he acted on a subconscious level to sabotage his own life.

CHAPTER 3

Star Symbols

 s we have seen, dream symbols cannot have set meanings, as they vary markedly in how people perceive them. An astrological birth chart, in contrast, is constructed around the time, date and place of the subject's birth, and these factors influence the interpretation of the symbols. As Jung pointed out, things born of the moment reflect the qualities of the moment.

Through her work as an astrologer, Helen has come to see that the birth chart lays out in blueprint form exactly how our energy fields interact and how we tend to see the world around and within ourselves. It also reveals how we perceive the many people in our lives, such as mother, father, grandparents, children, friends and lovers. Using the chart, we can understand how our perceptions of others may actually affect them on an energy level. It is quite common for people to begin to behave in the way we expect them to.

If we dream of a particular person, by aligning the chart in the right way, we can deduce which of our energies may need attention. The people we dream about act as indicators of how we are handling our lives. Our perceptions of them, and what we project on to them, can give us valuable information about how our internal energies are working.

If someone we know quite well, such as an aunt or a cousin, or indeed, a close friend, loses their job, or falls ill, or if we dream of these things happening to them, we can trace this imbalance back to ourselves and find out which area of ourselves is out of alignment.

Similarly, certain objects, plants and animals have strong meanings for different people, and when these symbols recur both in life and dreams, this can signal a need for change or warn of changes to come.

When attempting to interpret a dream through the medium of the birth chart, the first thing to do is to isolate the scene or the kind of action in the dream, which will give vital clues as to where in the chart to begin looking. This can be quite difficult to ascertain at first, as it is essential to define the main emphasis of the dream, and not be distracted by a particular symbol at the expense of the overall message. Once the correct point of focus has been identified, other aspects of the dream naturally fall into place.

This does not necessarily mean that the message has been revealed, but that the overall context has been defined. For instance, a dream from our files featured two friends who shared the same kind of eyes. It might have been tempting immediately to concentrate on the eyes. However, the general context of the dream was that they were close friends, a factor which came under the seventh house. The dream therefore indicated that they shared a similar viewpoint.

In another dream, the basic action involved a kind of war, part of which was being fought in a town. There were soldiers running around and snipers firing at each other. The buildings of the town were made of pre-cast concrete. The person in the dream was trying to get away from the fighting and the dream eventually resolved itself when he ran along a bridge, looked over the side, grasped the top of a tall pine tree and swung himself down to the forest floor, where there was a feeling of complete and total peace.

Again, we might have been caught up in the symbolism of the soldiers, the snipers and the concrete, but, from an astrological viewpoint, the main theme of the dream was conflict and escaping from conflict. The idea of a conflict which had reached a crisis point led us, in this particular case, to the eighth house of the dreamer's chart, which represents change through crisis, transformation, death and rebirth, amongst other things. The eighth house was found to contain two oppositions, and we saw at once that the dreamer was trying to find a way to deal with the conflicting energies which quite often brought disharmony in his life.

Another interesting parallel came to light. The dreamer walked to the centre of a bridge (astrologically, oppositions are shown by a straight line joining the two opposing planets), swung down and landed in a place of complete peace. In terms of the dreamer's horoscope, the place of peace was represented by the centre of the chart, which symbolizes the still centre of being, the place where we are grounded and no longer pulled about by conflicting aims and motives. So the dream was showing the dreamer how to experience this deep inner peace by finding the point of stillness within himself.

To take another example of how dreams can be keyed into the chart, a friend of Helen's dreamed that her front teeth were crumbling away, and either disappeared, or looked like 'shells of teeth'. In the chart, physical appearance comes under the auspices of the first house. Although Helen's friend had a Sagittarius ascendant, Saturn was in Capricorn in the first house, indicating that it was with this particular principle that the trouble lay.

Saturn represents discipline, structure and the setting of specific boundaries. The teeth, in astrology, are symbolically related to Saturn. Analysing the dream from an astrological perspective, we suggested that the subject was not setting enough boundaries for herself, and perhaps not letting others know when they had stepped into her personal space. She agreed that her authority was crumbling, as she tends to let others take advantage of her kind and easygoing nature.

It is necessary when interpreting dreams in this way to have an understanding of how the signs, planets and houses of the chart relate to different categories of symbolism and mythology. Take the Sun, for example. It symbolizes the self, the ego, creativity, how we shine, how we can best express our creative energy, sunflowers and gold; these are just some of the many correspondences which can be traced to this symbol. The Moon, on the other hand, symbolizes how we react, our nurturing and mothering nature and silver, for instance, while the sign Aries represents the thrust of new life, new beginnings and the urge to get things out from the unmanifest to the manifest.

It is important to stress that, even though these different categories have specific symbols, the way they are perceived varies dramatically according to the date, time and place of birth of the individual concerned.

Interestingly, when fairly long and involved dreams are analysed astrologically, certain scenes within them quite often highlight, through association, the same houses, or bring one back to the same planetary sequences, as though to underline specific patterns within the chart.

When no apparent theme can be found in the dream, or the action is particularly surreal or obscure, it may be difficult to key the dream into the chart.

In another dream from our files, the dreamer (a woman) was standing on the roof of her house while a buffalo jumped repeatedly over her head. The dream conveyed an impression of the absurd or surreal, and it was hard not only to find any kind of background theme, but to discern which of the symbols was most relevant. Taking the person as the theme led us to the first house of the chart and we were then guided to find out how she projected herself into her environment.

Jupiter, the dreamer's ruling planet, being close to the Sagittarian ascendant suggested a person who liked to be open to new and mind-expanding experiences and disliked being restricted or pinned down. Perhaps this was why she was on the roof. However, the image of the buffalo repeatedly jumping over her head could have been an expression of aggression directed at herself, a form of self-sabotage or a constant threat. More playfully, it might have been linked to the cow jumping over the moon in the nursery rhyme.

In instances like this, the flow-chart system is invaluable, as it enables dream symbols to be identified and cross-referenced, and the underlying theme to be discovered from the links between the symbols. This information can then be slotted into the natal chart, or aligned with current transits or progressions.

Another interesting factor about this way of analysing dreams is that the dream material gives a firsthand account of how the various parts of the psyche are functioning, which may not be immediately apparent to the astrologer or the client, as it comes from a deep subconscious level.

For instance, the client's dream on page 146 reveals a chronic lack of self-esteem. Although various factors in the chart clearly show this, an astrologer could not easily ascertain the extent to which the client has managed to overcome or heal certain difficult planetary placements during her life.

Astrologers cannot form an accurate picture of how far their clients have evolved and how much work they have done on the issues in their charts, although it is possible to get some idea by studying the various transits and progressions. Unless clients own up, during a consultation, that they still suffer from a certain problem, the astrologer can only make an educated guess. This is where the information given in the dream is so valuable: it highlights the reality of the client's inner life, without pretence or glossing over the situation.

By tying together the dream and the chart, we find out which areas of our lives need the most attention and gain a kind of running commentary, alerting us to areas where we are becoming unbalanced, or acting as our own worst enemy. This can assist the process of self-development, because it shows what progress we are making and reveals the next step on the path.

As a further example, a person dreamed that she was driving her yellow car along a road, and moving forward quite smoothly. As she rounded a bend, she came across a sheet of lead or similar metal as high as a two-storey house, completely wedged across the road at a junction. It blocked off the left side of the road, stopping her from proceeding on her journey. However, by manoeuvring around two white bollards in the middle of the road, she managed to turn the car around, move across to the other side and make her turn, even though this might have been dangerous or illegal.

At first glance this might have appeared to be a warning dream, telling the dreamer that there could be obstacles to pursuing a certain path, but that, with some difficult and risky manipulation, her goal could be achieved.

Astrologically, a short local journey comes under the third house, which relates to communications, exchange of information and the way we use our minds. This section of the dreamer's chart was ruled by the sign Virgo, which is quite a discriminating and mentalistic sign, and also by Mercury, which was situated in Taurus, in the section related to career goals, authority, and public image.

This introduced the idea that the dream was about progress in the subject's career, and also about her public image, being an authority on a certain subject, and attitudes to others in authoritarian positions.

The image of grey metal as an obstacle in her path revealed a Saturnine influence. Saturn shows us the areas where we feel inadequate, have fears which may need to be worked through, or tend to block ourselves. In this case, Saturn was placed in Sagittarius, in the section of the chart connected with attitudes to work, daily routine and health. It also formed a grand trine to Pluto in Virgo and Mercury in Taurus.

Trines are aspects of relative ease, but they often denote an area of the chart where a behaviour pattern has become entrenched. Having both Saturn and Pluto as part of a grand trine in a sense emphasized a heavy, very studious and somewhat critical and over-perfectionist attitude.

With Mercury in Taurus, the dreamer was realistic about the problems connected with any potential career move; the added weight of both Saturn and Pluto meant that her mind tended to be overly negative, self-critical and doubting of its own ability to succeed, chiefly because of its perfectionist attitude. There was a feeling of: 'If I can't be perfect, I won't attempt it.'

The dream had, so far, revealed the subject's tendency to think in a negative way about moving forward, succeeding or assuming authority. The dreamer then described how she realized that she could turn back on to the other side of the road, which showed the need for a U-turn in the way she reacted, a change to a more positive mode of thinking. Even though it might be risky, she should take the path she wanted to take.

One last point: the car she was driving was a yellow car, and yellow is quite often associated with Gemini and with mental ability, intellect and the mind. So the dream was telling her that stopping herself from doing something, because of her over-critical mental attitude, was a typical day's mental journey.

The way in which people are positioned in a dream is quite often reflected by the actual position of the planets on the dreamer's chart.

In Joan's dream (discussed in more detail on pages 146–158), she was sitting at a table between two men, at an equal distance from her. The character and appearance of the men, and what they say, reflect perfectly two planets placed at equidistant angles to the Moon in her chart. Similarly, in the dream interpreted in Chapter 1, Sue found herself in a queue, and this was reflected by a stellium, or queue of planets, in her chart.

Such striking illustrations of Jung's theory of synchronicity (or meaningful coincidences) crop up surprisingly often, even when the dreamer knows little or nothing about astrology, or has no idea which planetary transits or progressions are currently in motion. Strange dream images can also be mirrored by combinations of energies in the chart. Everything in the chart is an expression of a certain kind of energy.

For example, natal energies such as Mars in Libra, where the natural aggressive thrust of Mars is tempered by a consideration for others, could be represented in a dream as a harmonious room, with strategic blobs of red paint here and there. Alternatively, there might be two people pulling a red piece of cloth between them, each one trying to claim it for themselves. The subject might dream of attempting to achieve some goal and being continually put off by other people's ideas, wishes or comments. The possibilities are as endless as the expression of such energies in daily life.

Some people with Mars in Libra may, in their daily lives, always consider things from a several viewpoints, or become indignant at injustice to others. On a more negative note, they may be married to someone with whom they constantly argue.

As another example, having Saturn in Leo, square Moon in Capricorn, would probably result in problems of self-confidence, perhaps compounded by a difficult childhood lacking in love. This could be symbolized by dream images such as a child hemmed in by stone blocks.

Considering the innate wisdom of the subconscious mind, some of the many other astrological features, including asteroids and fixed stars, may be represented in dreams too. We cannot provide a comprehensive list of possible symbols for each astrological feature here, but we would like to encourage you to carry out your own research in this field.

CHAPTER 4

Dream States

 hy do we dream? Nobody knows the full answer to that question. The conventional, but unsatisfactory, explanation is that dreams act rather like a computer taking unnecessary material 'off line', in that they sift through the day's experiences and discard whatever is unnecessary. First put forward in 1866 by Robert, a Frenchman, this theory was published by Evans and Newman in the *New Scientist* in 1964 and gained widespread acceptance.

Evans and Newman were responding to the belief that dreams were necessary to maintain sanity, a misconception which is still perpetuated. This erroneous theory probably arose from some questionable experiments on cats. The hapless creatures were floated on planks of wood in water. Each time they nodded off, their heads would touch the water, thus depriving them of sleep – and not just dreaming sleep, as was implied. Unsurprisingly, the cats eventually demonstrated aggressive behaviour.

There is actually no evidence to suggest that we need to dream at all. On the contrary, it would seem that dreams are something of a luxury. This is supported by the fact that some modern antidepressant drugs eliminate dreaming, or rapid-eye movement (REM) sleep completely, yet the patients taking these drugs display no detrimental effects whatsoever.

It is feasible that a proportion of dreams, particularly the less memorable ones, do serve as a sort of filing-system purpose, although this hypothesis remains pure conjecture. However, if the sole function of dreams were to sort data, they would not be so easily contaminated by external stimuli.

For example, imagine that someone is having a dream which reflects the events of the previous day. Then, suddenly, the sound of a neighbour mowing his or her grass (in real life) infiltrates the dreamer's unconscious mind. The dream will almost certainly change very quickly to incorporate this noise in some way and might then take a new tack altogether. Evans and Newman's idea does not account for this eventuality.

Why should dreams reflect events from previous centuries, or be set in alien landscapes, if they are merely discarding useless information as no longer wanted? Why do some unfortunate people experience horrific, recurring or varied nightmares, sometimes two or three times a week? It seems unreasonable to assume that they are merely processing unwanted memories. These are just a few of the facts that contradict accepted scientific theories about dreams.

Certain phenomena which can occur during dreaming sleep – hypnagogic imagery, lucid dreams, false awakenings and sleep paralysis – disprove beyond all doubt Evans and Newman's theory, and demonstrate that dreams serve a number of purposes.

Hypnagogic imagery

Hypnagogic imagery occurs at onset of sleep (during Stage 1 sleep), when the subject is hovering somewhere between consciousness and slumber. Those who are able to experience wakeful visual imagery may observe phantom-like figures, or even clear pictures. Many report seeing an eye gazing at them for long periods of time. Conversations are often heard, sometimes in a foreign language unfamiliar to the subject.

Lucid dreams

A lucid dream is when the subject actually becomes aware of dreaming. At that point, long-term memory and full identity are restored. In effect, full waking consciousness is achieved within the dream. Moreover, the dream can be controlled and manipulated at will.

In 1975 Dr Keith Hearne managed to obtain structured communication from a dreaming subject, thus creating a link between this material world and another state of being, a level of existence where anything is possible. This discovery introduced a new science and provided the opportunity to study the inner universe. Now more than 30 universities around the world are researching lucid dreams, which seem to offer enormous potential for stress relief, healing and grief therapy, for instance.

A lucid dream can be so striking that the dreamer is unable to distinguish it from conscious reality, and this poses a number of questions. Is the lucid dream another level of reality, or is full consciousness just a convincing dream state? Do we exist on more than one level or dimension of reality?

These questions led Dr Hearne on to speculate that perhaps we all exist in a mentalistic universe, in a reality created by thought. This would explain countless anomalies and apparently unanswerable questions, particularly if it were linked with quantum theory, the concept of God, and modern discoveries in the field of virtual reality.

Essentially, quantum theory deals with science on the very edge of the physical universe, at the door of infinity. To put it very simply, it proposes that, at a sub-atomic level, matter vibrates at such an incredible speed that it literally exists in two places at the same time.

As we are made up of sub-atomic particles, which all vibrate at that same incredible speed, it follows that all matter must exist in two places at the same time. So, for every source of energy, there exists a double. However, quantum theory also suggests that each double must also have a double, and so on. In other words, we live in a perpetuating cycle of multiple existence, or an unknown number of universes or dimensions.

To follow this through to its natural conclusion, because we are all made up of atoms, with space between each one, we are merely a source of cohesive energy. On a sub-atomic level, we do not exist as physical entities, but as energy.

In effect, the brain maintains a permanent electrical field (permanent, that is, until death of the physical body) and the process of thought is contained within this electrical field. The brain's electrical activity can be seen to be stimulated by a single thought, which indicates that thought might be a form of electrical energy.

As energy cannot be destroyed, it must be assumed that thoughts are converted into something else or – according to quantum theory – to somewhere else, or both. Therefore, thought might also exist in two places at once. Because we are merely a cohesive source of energy ourselves, we too could be the product of thought.

Designers of virtual-reality systems maintain that we are on the verge of creating the ultimate illusion in this field, where the user will not be able to distinguish between the two levels of existence. Perhaps we already exist in the most powerful virtual-reality system the mind could conceive, a system invented in a mentalistic universe, a universe of thought created by God.

If so, anything is possible. It would certainly explain many curious inconsistencies, such as telepathy, precognitive dreams and premonitions, where – turning science around on its head – the effect precedes the cause. It would also seem feasible that the principles and energies of astrology could have a very real effect on our everyday lives.

False awakenings

In a false awakening, we dream that we have woken. This phenomenon is closely related to the lucid dream, the difference being that the false awakening is not recognized by the subject.

Many people believe that they suffer from insomnia. However, Dr Hearne's work has revealed that some are simply dreaming of waking during the night. It is possible that a large proportion of the population experience this phenomenon without realizing it.

There are those who dream of waking up, looking at the clock, or turning over and going back to sleep. In reality, the brainwave monitor sometimes proves that such subjects are still in REM sleep. In each case, the experience has been an elaborate illusion.

A false awakening is often triggered by an anticipated interruption of sleep. For example, a person might believe that their alarm has gone off, only to discover that it was a dream when the alarm really does ring.

If a false awakening is recognized, it can be utilized to initiate a lucid dream. This is where full advantage can be taken of the phenomenon of the light-switch effect. For instance, if a subject wakes and turns on a light successfully, this constitutes proof that they are awake. However, if the light fails to function, there is reason to suspect that they are dreaming. As soon as they think they may be dreaming, lucidity ensues.

Sleep paralysis

Sleep paralysis is an entirely different matter. This curious condition is probably responsible for many reports of ghost or spirit hauntings. If one is not familiar with the experience, it can be very disturbing. Some people who undergo sleep paralysis believe that they are dying.

This strange state always occurs on the edge between REM sleep and consciousness and, again, dreamers are absolutely convinced that they are wide awake. Nevertheless, their brainwave pattern will indicate that they are in fact dreaming.

Subjects usually believe they have woken up in a state of total paralysis, although they are actually in REM sleep, during which, apart from the respiratory system and the eyes, the muscles of the body are unable to function.

In addition, they may report seeing spectres, sensing a presence in the room, or the imminent approach of something or somebody. At this point, they generally panic and try to break free from the grip of the paralysis. Unfortunately, the more they fight the condition, the more exhausted they will become.

The secret is to recognize and accept that it is a dream and be content to lie still. The condition will soon pass and they will either wake up or drift back into a conventional dream; there is no need to be afraid.

In 1996, a woman experiencing sleep paralysis was convinced that the devil was licking her neck. This terrifying delusion resulted in her hair turning white. If she had been familiar with the condition, her awful ordeal could have been averted.

✳ ✳ ✳

Taking into account these not uncommon variations of the dream, it is evident that dismissing dreams as merely a method of processing surplus data is too much of a generalization. The purpose of dreaming is far more complex.

Finally, there is a common misconception that dreams last only for a fleeting moment. 'They're over in a flash!' is a remark often heard. The idea gained credence during the nineteenth century after a Frenchman, named Maury, reported a lengthy dream which culminated in his own death by guillotine. Maury awoke, recalling how the blade had fallen, to discover that his bed had collapsed across his neck. He reasoned (logically enough) that although the dream had seemed a long one, it must have taken place in an instant.

However, as dreams are open to contamination by outside influences, it is possible that Maury's bed had been making warning noises before it collapsed, and perhaps it was not the first time this had happened. Alternatively, maybe the bed had caved in some time before Maury awoke. Unfortunately, we will never be able to establish the facts of the case.

Using sophisticated monitoring equipment, Dr Hearne has proved that dreams occur in real time. In other words, if you dream of an event which takes a minute, you can be sure that about a minute will have passed in the material world.

CHAPTER 5

Dreamscapes

n this chapter we will demonstrate how dreamscapes (the settings of dreams) are closely allied to the houses of the astrological chart and dictate the tone of the interpretation. When a dreamscape is viewed in the context of the dreamer's circumstances, a dream which seems enigmatic generally becomes easier to interpret.

The analyst will always begin by first trying to isolate the underlying theme of a dream, and will then look at the images linked to the twelve houses of the chart in order to work out how these tie into different dream sequences.

The Twelve Houses of the Chart

As the different houses of the chart contain quite a lot of varied symbolism, we shall summarize the essential meanings and symbols of each house, so that they can be more easily linked with dream images.

The first house

The first house of the chart is traditionally connected with the kind of impression people form when they first meet us: our persona, or outer personality. It also relates to the various ways in which we protect ourselves from other people's actions or scrutiny, and to our physical appearance and how we see ourselves.

Denoting an underlying quality of energy which permeates the actual act of self-expression, the essential purpose of the first house is to act as a link between our inner motives and desires and our outer connection with the environment. It is rather like the middle point in the symbol for infinity '∞'. Here, like Janus, we have one face turned inwards and the other outwards, to meet the world. This is the point at which we mediate between inner and outer energies.

Any dreams connected to issues of identity, to seeing oneself or one's face in a certain way (the dreamer in Chapter 3, for example, whose teeth were crumbling) can be associated with this section of the chart, as can dreams relating to physical changes or distortions.

The second house

The second house of the chart is allied to our personal possessions and finances, sense of security and value system. It also ties in with such issues as self-worth, or the lack of it. It is a strong indicator of the kinds of people, objects or experiences we value, materially, spiritually or emotionally.

Therefore, dreams pertaining to the second house may relate to such issues as security, self-worth, value judgements, moral decisions and attitudes to money and affairs.

The third house

The third house of the chart concerns the way we take in information from the environment and relay it out again: how we communicate with others, how we think, any mental blocks we may have. It is connected with our early years at school, and our attitude to learning and teaching. It also has a bearing on short trips and various modes of transport as well as neighbours, the local area and our brothers and sisters.

Any dreams featuring such subjects may be related to this house and offer valuable insights about our state of mind, and how we habitually think and communicate.

The fourth house

The fourth house of the chart is associated with home and domestic matters, and issues surrounding nurturing (how we nurture others and the nurturing we received as children). It shows how we meet our own needs, or where we adopt a parenting role. It also concerns underground places like mines and graves, throws light on our old age, and has links with real estate, land, agriculture and gardening.

Dreams connected to this house may feature parental attitudes, images of the mother or father, childhood, or any of the above subjects. This house, like the other water houses (the eighth and the twelfth) usually indicates deep involvement, especially in terms of ancestral or hereditary traits, or issues from past lives.

The fifth house

The fifth house of the chart relates to creativity, self-expression, children, pleasure, leisure and risk-taking. It is also relevant to setting up in business and speculation, and is connected with the theatre, entertainment, love as experienced in childhood and our capacity to give and receive love.

Dreams linked to this house may also deal with problems of confidence, as the fifth house tends to show how confident we are about ourselves and what we create. Dreams about taking a risk, being on stage, children, etc. will probably fit in here. Likely scenarios would be playschools and theatres, for example.

The sixth house

The sixth house of the chart is connected to diet and health, our daily routine and habits, attitudes to work, people at work, staff and employees. It also concerns the mind–body synthesis, how our mental state affects our body.

Dreams about our jobs, work colleagues, illness, dietary or any other habits, such as tea-drinking and smoking, are generally linked to the sixth house.

The seventh house

The seventh house of the chart is associated with our relationships, not only in terms of love and marriage, but also with close

friends and grandparents, as well as contact with the public, contracts or agreements in general, and bitter enemies. This is the
house of the psychological shadow, too.

Any dreams connected to this house would be about our relationships, marriage, or people we dislike or even despise. Dreams
in which we, or others, initiate a deal or a contract would also fit
in here, as would dreams about social arrangements.

The eighth house

The eighth house of the chart is concerned with change and
transformation, including such things as birth, sex, death, secrets,
metaphysical or paranormal studies, soul mates and deep one-to-
one emotional bonds. It is also related to other people's money,
taxes, inheritances, the family fortune, banks, loans and debts
and, finally, crisis.

Dreams allied to this sector of the chart may well include
powerful scenarios of death and rebirth, irrevocable endings,
conflict and legacies.

The ninth house

The ninth house of the chart relates to broadening our horizons,
anything which takes us out of our ordinary, everyday life and
places us in new surroundings, such as a trip abroad or exploring
a new level of consciousness. This sector also encompasses travel
and foreign countries, higher education, beliefs (religious or otherwise) and the law. In addition, it has a lot to do with the
publishing business, in-laws and gurus.

Dreams connected with this sector could involve any combination of the above subjects, and would also include images of the
archetypal wise old man or woman who guides us out of trouble.

The tenth house

The tenth house of the chart is associated with careers and our
public image, how other people see us. It refers to authority
figures, people who seem to have power over us, such as fathers,

dictatorial mothers, the government or the bank manager, and to how we are regarded by the community in general.

Dreams relating to this sector would concern people who control us, or the kind of authority we ourselves command. Any issues referring to career changes, or moving forward in life, belong to this category, as do the sorts of dream where we are standing naked in a public place and everyone is looking at us.

The eleventh house

The eleventh house is connected with our ideals, dreams and aspirations, our friends and associates, peer groups, and clubs or organizations which reflect our interests. It is also allied to social situations and serving the community.

Dreams which reflect this house relate to our connections with society, any wild dreams or urges we may have, friends (but not our close friends), and so on. These dreams often reveal our role in society.

The twelfth house

The twelfth house concerns anything to do with the unconscious or subconscious mind, spiritual or mystical qualities, with helping or serving others, and self-abnegation. It also links with social institutions such as hospitals, asylums, prisons and homes of various kinds. This sector of the chart alerts us to the characteristics that create problems for us, and any tendency we have to act as our own worst enemy.

Dreams connected with this house, the house of dreams itself, may be very vivid and colourful, and concern mystical or spiritual subjects. Paradoxically, these dreams often involve being trapped, in prison, or any other of the institutions mentioned above. They may also highlight areas where we are acting the martyr, or sacrificing a part of ourselves for some other goal, or for someone else. Past-life dreams can also be linked to this house if the symbolism is appropriate.

* * *

Having quickly run through the twelve houses of the chart indicating the areas which each covers, and the possible dream subjects appropriate to each, we shall look at the significance of the sign in the context of the houses.

For instance, some people with Scorpio on the cusp of the second house in their charts might tend to derive a sense of power from their possessions. They might use material goods or money to bargain, or have deep-seated problems in connection with self-worth and allowing money energy to flow into their lives.

Certain persons with Leo on the cusp of the second house might have an egotistical attitude to their possessions, and identify with them. Thus their egos would be severely affected if, say, a prize car was damaged, or if they were poor and could not afford to buy lavish presents for their friends and relations.

So, if someone from the first group dreams of owning a new car, we can immediately link this to a sense of power; they may be using this car to go one better than their peers, to impress people, or as a bargaining tool.

If a person from the second group dreams of owning a new car, on the other hand, this would relate directly to their ego. The car would become an extension of themselves, and if anyone criticized it, or professed dislike of that particular model, the dreamer would be likely to take it as a personal insult.

As another illustration, those with Sagittarius on the cusp of the fifth house would be inclined to turn to their natural sense of adventure in order to have fun and use their leisure time to make them feel good. Those with Virgo on the cusp of the fifth house, however, would perhaps prefer to spend their leisure time occupied with a meticulous pursuit such as building model boats or planes, or embroidering intricate patterns.

If a person from the first group dreams that someone is telling them they need to have more fun and excitement, they would take this to mean regaining a sense of adventure, getting out into open spaces again and enjoying the fresh air, because they have probably been too restricted.

To subjects of the second group, the same dream would have a very different meaning. For them, fun might be related less to the outdoor life than to making something intricate, beautiful and functional. Alternatively, it might take the form of mastering a new skill or craft, such as playing a muscial instrument.

So the information the signs give to the houses provides a much more detailed scenario from which the dream setting can be identified and related to the relevant section of the chart. Next we will take a look at a few actual dreamscapes and see how they fit in with the various houses of the chart.

In one of the dreams from our files the dreamer found herself on the edge of a forest, digging in the earth with her bare hands. She uncovered two carved wooden heads of goddesses. They were beautifully fashioned out of natural wood, in a kind of semi-profile, with flat backs, as though intended to be placed on a wall. She picked up one to take with her and left the other, burying it in the earth again. Rounding a corner a little further into the wood, she came across a natural grove. A small doll-shaped goddess figure dressed in a bright red flamenco-type dress stood in a shrine made of wood and branches. At the foot of the statue were heaps of different-coloured polished gemstones. The dreamer took a handful of the stones and then woke up.

Close consideration of the natural setting of the dream and the symbolism of the act of finding and digging up something from the earth, especially such objects as the heads of goddesses, nurturers and providers, immediately led us to the fourth house of the chart, which is particularly concerned with the earth, and things of the earth.

In this person's chart we found Libra on the cusp of the fourth house. Libra, having a lot to do with harmony and beauty, tied in with the description of the skilfully carved heads of the goddesses. The continuing theme of the goddess was emphasized when the statue was discovered in the shrine, which again expressed the mother/all-provider theme, and showed that we were on track by stressing this point.

Having found the section of the chart to which the dream related, we could confidently begin to tie in the other symbols connected with the house, sign, ruler of the sign, position and aspects to ruler, and expand on all the other clues.

In this instance, Venus, the ruler of Libra, was situated in Aquarius in the eighth house of the chart and in direct opposition to Pluto, which was conjunct the IC, while Venus was conjunct the MC (see page 170). We could now conclude that this dream referred to a change in life path, and that the effect of that change would not only be connected to the earth, but would be very profound, long lasting and irrevocable, and also bring nurturing and fulfilment.

The red dress of the third goddess indicated the planet Mars, which was also situated in the eighth house and was in opposition to Uranus. The statue was dressed rather like a flamenco dancer. Mars/Uranus produces a very high energy, which needs to be used, otherwise its effects can turn in on one as suppressed energy, possibly causing ill-health.

The sudden appearance of the goddess in that bright red flamenco dress signified an understanding of and an ability to use this powerful energy in a beneficial way and express it fully. This particular kind of high energy as represented by Mars and Uranus is similar to that of Shiva Nataraja, Lord of the Dance. Indeed, in India, red is the colour of Shakti, who is the female counterpart of Shiva. Shakti symbolizes female energy, the energy within everything, which is in continuous motion; this is the force which creates, maintains and dissolves the universe. It is also known as Kundalini Shakti.

By focusing on the correct section of the dreamer's chart, we discovered the meaning of her dream. It signalled a change of direction and a coming into power, this power having continuous growth built into it, and bestowing the ability to heal and to transform certain aspects of nature.

We have not given the entire analysis of the dream, but enough to show how, once the underlying theme and the main thrust of the interpretation have been established, the deeper symbolic aspects can be examined in greater detail.

In India, they have a saying that you use a thorn to remove a thorn. This is like interpreting dreams with the birth chart, in that you are using the unique symbolism of the chart to decode the unique symbolism of the dream, yet the two are related: they both equate to that particular person's way of perceiving the universe.

Another short dream from our files was set in a shoe shop. The subject entered the shop and the owner, who was busy serving a customer, said to the dreamer, 'You have to look out for the ones that try to drain you.'

A salesman's job is to serve others; in this particular person's chart attitudes to service, which is a sixth-house characteristic, were ruled by Sagittarius, the sign on the cusp of the sixth house, and Saturn was situated in the sixth house in Sagittarius. This in itself pointed to difficulties in attitudes to work connected with being confined and needing freedom and space. Perhaps the dreamer needed to find the right job, one that would give sufficient freedom for growth without cramping their spirit and need for adventure.

However, the main theme centred on the advice given by the salesman about people who 'try to drain you'. Draining and being drained are associated with the planet Neptune. In this particular case, having Neptune conjunct Jupiter, the ruler of the sixth house, in the dreamer's chart indicated a vulnerability to sob stories. These two planets together gave a very Piscean feel, denoting the sort of person who attracts those in need of help.

The meaning of the dream appeared to be linked to performing some kind of service. The dreamer had to have enough space, not feel too cramped, and had also to watch out for those people who, as hangers-on, would drain vital energy.

There was another interesting point to consider. The sixth house is also the section of the chart which relates to health, so, if the dream's message was heeded, the subject's health and energy levels would improve.

Again, this is a very basic interpretation and we have not gone into the reasons why it was a shoe shop, as opposed to a dress shop, for example (perhaps the dreamer felt downtrodden or worn out). This line of enquiry would highlight other important points central to the overall meaning.

The Four Elements

Another facet of dreamscapes is that of the four elements: earth, air, fire and water. Sometimes people dream of flying through the air, being engulfed by water, surrounded by fire, or being buried in the earth.

All the elements relate astrologically to our different functions and ways of perceiving the world. Air is linked to the mental function, water to the emotions, fire to the spirit, creativity and intuition, and earth to sensation, to the practical necessities of life.

We tend to use one or two of these four functions more than the others and are therefore underdeveloped in at least two of them. For example, a person may rely on a combination of the elements of fire (spirit and intuition) and air (thought and deatched perception and logic), in the process neglecting feeling and sensation. Another common blend is earth (practical realism) with water (sensitivity and feeling), leaving fire and air as inferior functions.

Some dreams about the elements may be attempts to redress such imbalances and issue a warning, perhaps that we are too realistic or not sufficiently down-to-earth.

In one dream from our files, the subject described how she found herself moving through a series of swimming pools. A voice was saying, 'There's too much water, there's too much water.' In fact, this subject was overly-sensitive to many things, which was detrimental to her, as it inhibited her from acting as positively as she might have done had she been more thick-skinned. Where the element of water is dominant, the person is generally too easily influenced and will find it difficult to see things from a detached perspective.

Each of the houses of the chart relates to one of the elements, and this is another way in which dreams can be linked into a natal chart. It is also possible that connections can be made via the different signs of the zodiac which also relate to the four elements, but this will depend on the dream scenario.

We can use the content and nature of the dream, the features which form the dreamscape, to link into the chart. Then the symbolism in the chart can help us to decipher or bring to the surface other elements which shed new light on the overall interpretation. When we connect dream symbolism with the chart, the benefits of both systems combine to bring us life-changing aid and advice.

CHAPTER 6

The Darker Side

f you were asked to list the positive and negative aspects of your character, how easy would you find the task? You might be able to highlight one or two of your better attributes without difficulty, but how do you think you would fare if you were asked to write an essay which focused entirely on a single facet of your darker side?

Everybody possesses more unsavoury character traits than they care to admit. For example, they may say, 'I know that I can be a bit intimidating sometimes, but that's just me.' Or, 'If people can't take me as I am, that's their problem.'

When such statements are made in connection with negative characteristics, they are often a form of denial. To a certain extent, everybody has the capacity to switch off, rather than see themselves as they truly are, warts and all.

Some people are shocked when, having unwittingly been caught on video, they watch themselves displaying the less pleasant side of their characters. 'That's not me,' is a fairly common response, until they take a closer look. Then there is often silence and embarrassment as they see themselves, for the first time in a true light.

A reasonable degree of self-awareness, including an acknowledgement of our negative character traits, is extremely helpful in dream interpretation. To achieve a high level of accuracy, the analyst needs to know something about the subject of the dreams – a brief psychological profile, at least. Without this information, only a general interpretation can be made, which may or may not be accurate.

For example, imagine that the subject dreams about a fox sneaking up on an unsuspecting prey. If he has described himself (truthfully) as a fairly young and ambitious high-flyer, willing to do anything to further his own career, straight away the analyst is given a clue as to where the interpretation might lead. It may transpire that, in waking life, the dreamer is approaching a situation where he is prepared to behave in a less than creditable manner to achieve a goal.

However, if asked to analyse his own dream, a less self-aware high-flyer would be likely to ignore or deny the less pleasant side of his character and fabricate a result to fit the dream. He might take it as a warning that somebody else was slyly plotting against him, for instance. For accuracy in self-analysis, we must acknowledge our faults as well as our virtues.

One of David's own dreams illustrates this point very well. He hates leaving things until the last minute, especially when it comes to preparing manuscripts for publication. On this occasion, he had asked a friend – we'll call him Richard – to do some research for a magazine article he was writing. Richard, an expert in a scientific field in which David had only limited experience, is a very busy person and was doing the work as a favour. However, David remembered that, through no fault of his own, Richard had once kept him waiting when they were due to attend a social event.

This memory had haunted David and, although he had plenty of time in which to do the work, he found himself calling his friend fairly frequently to enquire how far he had progressed with it. Although Richard gave him no reason to suspect that he was annoyed, David had a dream which alerted him to the fact that he was becoming a pest.

In the dream he was cramped inside a telephone box (i.e. a place of communication) with a man who was trying to write a letter. Each time he began to write, David snatched the page from his hand to read it. After a few attempts, the man gave up, pushed his way out of the telephone box and told David to write his own letter.

When he had drawn up several flow charts and viewed the dream in its entirety, it became clear to David that he wasn't giving Richard the room or the time to fulfil his task without feeling under pressure. Being aware of his negative character trait of impatience, he backed off and, despite his urge to check up on the progress of the work, he resisted calling Richard again. Soon afterwards, much to David's relief, he received the material, well within the allotted time.

Although Richard was too polite to tell him he was becoming tiresome, the dream warned David that he might end up researching some very complex material for himself. If he had not acknowledged the negative side of his personality, he would never have arrived at an accurate interpretation of his dream and curbed his impatience.

Guided Imagery

There are several techniques designed to aid the process of self-discovery and many books have been written about it. One of the most efficient approaches is to employ guided imagery, which is not to be confused with other forms of imagery.

Guided imagery for self-discovery is all about creating animated day-dreams which feature yourself in a problematical situation and allowing these visions to develop until a concluding scenario is reached. The results are then studied to discover whether a different approach could have led to a more successful outcome. This provides a perfect opportunity for self-criticism.

Some people may find it difficult to visualize themselves in this way. Let us study a hypothetical example in order to overcome this problem.

First, call to mind any problematical situation which requires a solution. (This need not be a problem of your own; it can be a complete fabrication.) Next, sit down with a notepad and pencil in a comfortable chair, in softly lit surroundings. Try to make sure you will not be disturbed. Then imagine a person, an animal or even an object to act as you in the day-dream. It might be a fictional or cartoon character, for example.

Suppose that the problem concerns a territorial dispute. It could take place in any setting, so let us assume that it centres on two broody chickens who both want to lay their eggs in the most prestigious nest-box.

You must decide what part you are to play in this dispute: one of the chickens, a cockerel, a farmer, even the nest-box, or any thing or person you like. Let us pretend that you choose to be the cockerel. Visualize the cockerel; take your time and study it in depth. Once you have a clear picture of its appearance and personality, bring your conscious thoughts back to reality, and write a detailed description of the cockerel for later analysis.

Return to the day-dream and set the scene for the conflict. When you are satisfied, animate it – set it in motion – and watch the dispute unfold, allowing the characters to act as they will. In other words, apart from monitoring the situation, you do not interfere; your chosen character will represent you. When the vision has run its course, describe it on paper in as much detail as you can recall.

Whether the problem is solved or not is unimportant. It is the actions that your representative character takes that hold the key to self-discovery.

Let us return to the original notes made to describe the main character. This alone can bring surprising results. One person might have seen the cockerel as proud and strutting, with a threatening beak. Another might have visualized a smaller creature, softer in temperament, reluctant to intervene unless the hens are unable to come to an amicable solution between themselves.

The first example might imply that, in real life, the day-dreamer is somewhat pushy and overbearing, and could be quite prepared to impose severe punishment on those who do not see things in the same way. Conversely, the latter might be too soft and willing to accept responsibility only when all other avenues have been exhausted.

Remember, because this is an exercise to discover your negative character traits, these are likely to be prevalent in the vision. If, on the other hand, you are attempting to identify your positive qualities, these would probably be most in evidence.

Simply isolating the actions of the cockerel and asking why the creature behaved in whatever way it did can bring about a revelation concerning your character traits. However, it is just as important not to overlook but to pay close attention to the other characters in the day-dream.

For instance, let us imagine that the hens you have visualized are different in appearance, one rather dishevelled and the other neat and trim. If, in your day-dream, the male bird gave preferential treatment to the well-groomed chicken, this might indicate that, in real life, you regard people in a superficial way, perhaps judging others by the way they dress.

Once such connections are made and accepted as revealing one's nature, the important thing is to acknowledge them.

Guided imagery is an extremely versatile technique, lending itself to many other useful purposes, such as giving up smoking, easing stress and losing weight. Imagine an appropriate scenario and see what part the main character (you) plays; observe the interactions with the other characters and the arguments that are put forward. Then begin an analysis of the day-dream. The results can be very exciting and beneficial.

Unfortunately, some people are unable to generate any visual imagery at all, let alone create a day-dream. They are predominantly left-brain users, who base their lives largely on logic and generally cannot 'see' anything in their mind's eye.

Although the human skull represents a single chamber, in effect, it houses three separate brains: the primitive hindbrain, which is responsible for basic functions, and the left and right hemispheres, with which we are concerned here.

Each hemisphere functions entirely independently from the other. They even differ in the way in which information is processed. If they were not connected by a neural bridge (known as the corpus callosum) there would be no interaction between the left and right brain. Some fascinating experiments have been carried out on subjects whose neural bridge has, for various reasons, been severed. Although both hemispheres continue to function, their left hand literally doesn't know what the right is doing.

The corpus callosum allows both sides of the brain to be engaged and interact. Therefore, we are able to participate in activities that stimulate whichever hemisphere is required. Bearing this in mind, it is possible for an extreme left-brain dependent to utilize the right brain to facilitate a degree of limited, creative self-analysis.

As the right brain is allied to visual imagery, it also relates to creativity – and herein lies the clue. An extreme left-brain dependent person, such as a mathematician or a computer analyst perhaps, will tend to enjoy factual books rather than novels, and have trouble forming mental pictures of imaginary scenes (a right-brain activity).

Nevertheless, if they are given a task to perform which engages the right brain – say writing fiction – they may well be able to stage their own problematical situation, such as the one of the two chickens vying for one nest box. However, due to their lack of visual imagery, they will find it much easier to imagine a situation in which the conflict is acted out by people instead of cartoon characters or animals.

In addition, to provide a degree of compatibilty with the left brain, it is recommended that they begin by planning the whole scenario on paper. This will be a relatively easy task, because it involves interaction between both hemispheres, and logic must be employed, which should appeal to the left-brain user.

Let us take another example of a dispute over territory. This time we shall substitute humans for chickens. The goal is to overcome a quarrel between two men over a favourite chair. Suppose that the left-brain user who is planning the story elects to be a neutral third party, with the role of resolving the issue.

The subject should make notes about the dress, status, age, etc. of the fictional characters and provide a sketchy psychological profile for each one, including the main character, who will be representing them. Then the scene should be set: is the chair in a house, an office or a place of recreation, for example?

Next it must be decided how best to deal with the disagreement: with reasoned argument, force, compromise or by involving the authorities, etc. Then an effective method of imposing the final decision should be chosen. Any number of other relevant features can be incorporated in the plan.

Let us imagine that the main character is described as a suave, debonair, high-powered type. This may well indicate that the subject is somewhat conceited and over-ambitious. Even more data will surface from a reading of the plot, and setting, action, dialogue and emotion will also provide valuable clues.

This technique may not be as easy as guided imagery, but it should enable a left-brain dependent person to achieve similar results in the quest for self-knowledge. Whichever method is used, the results can be entertaining and, at the same time, the subject may learn some very valuable lessons about their psychological make-up. Give it a try!

In addition, either of the above techniques, when combined with an astrologically-based psychological profile, will result in a much more detailed picture of the subject's character traits.

CHAPTER 7

Genevieve's Dream

Dreams that involve complex symbolism or complicated interactions with others are particularly difficult to interpret. The dream interpretation which follows is an example of the holistic method, whereby enigmatic dreams can be interpreted and layers of meaning uncovered which might not have been revealed if either the astrological or analytical method had been used independently.

As mentioned earlier, when clients send us a dream to interpret, they often include some background information which (consciously or not) they suspect has a bearing on the dream. The experienced analyst will always take notice of any extra data and bear it in mind when analysing the dream. It usually transpires that such remarks are very pertinent to the dream message.

In this instance, in her letter, Genevieve, the next subject, included remarks before and after her description of the dream. For example, she stated that she had been going out with a man who had loaned her his word processor. She also had a friend called Margaret, who used to be politically radical. Then, following the dream, the writer stated that she and her boyfriend had agreed to split up, because their objectives and goals in life were different.

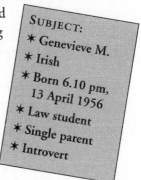

SUBJECT:
* Genevieve M.
* Irish
* Born 6.10 pm, 13 April 1956
* Law student
* Single parent
* Introvert

This information simplified the task of analysis and confirmed its accuracy for me as the subject's comments later clearly verified.

The Dream

✳ *In my dream, my friend, Margaret, was selling her word processor. The figure we agreed upon was £64. This figure was presented in bold type (£64 is the amount of my children's allowance and single-parent benefit).*

I wrote her a cheque for the correct sum, then discovered that I had already paid her for it, so asked for my cheque back. She refused. I threatened to phone the police, and when she still refused, I dialled 999.

A whole troop of policemen and women arrived. Ultimately, the police informed me that there was nothing they could do. I thought that I could take Margaret to court but, for an unknown reason, feared that the judge might conclude that the word processor was worth £64 times two.

After the police had left, I was in Margaret's storeroom. I took provisions which would amount to about £7. I thought I was getting some compensation for being cheated. On my way home, I passed a grocery store, and speculated that perhaps Margaret had wanted the money for some sort of political objective, and didn't care how she got it. ✳

Flow-chart Interpretation

The information Genevieve supplied about her boyfriend and Margaret proved very helpful with the interpretation. The dream is directly related to her recent liaison with her boyfriend.

When we see others in dreams, they may represent themselves, or, quite often, part of our own personality, the part that we might associate with the person about whom we dream. However, we have to look very closely before a decision can be made.

Studying this subject's dream as a whole, we found the same theme popping up time after time. There is no doubt that Margaret did not represent herself, but neither did she represent Genevieve. Instead, she represented specific aspects of Genevieve's boyfriend's character (the fact that it was Margaret's computer in the dream confirms this).

The description includes another clue as to what part of his character we are trying to identify. Viewed in its entirety, the dream indicates that we are dealing with his negative side. Genevieve's subconscious identified similar traits shared by her boyfriend and Margaret, traits her conscious mind might have missed. This makes it clear that the dream contains a message linked to the ending of their relationship.

The fact that Margaret was selling a word processor merely tells us that she represents the boyfriend (he had lent Genevieve a computer in real life). However, once the dream had started on this tack, it cleverly followed it through and continued to include the computer.

The fact Genevieve wanted to buy the computer, shows us that at the start of the relationship she was attracted to certain aspects of her boyfriend's personality. The dream quickly and ingeniously leads us through the relationship from beginning to end.

Agreeing to pay £64 – the sum total of her benefit – signifies that she put a lot into the relationship. However, she realized that she had paid twice (i.e. gave far more in the relationship than she was receiving). This is confirmed when Margaret refused to refund the money, which indicates that the boyfriend was perfectly content to let Genevieve put all the effort into the relationship, while he sat back, giving little in return.

She was the only one who could see what was going on. She felt that if she shared her concerns with him (in the dream, she involves the police), not only would he not understand, but he might even regard it as trivial or boring. Perhaps she had tried this approach and got a negative response.

She wondered about taking the matter to court, but thought that the judge might consider the machine worth twice the price. This suggests that she considered discussing her relationship with someone else. However, she feared that they would not understand and might say that if she wanted him, she had to give twice as much to the relationship as she got in return. She knew that another person would not understand her situation or see it as it really was.

And now we come to the part of the dream which demonstrates the strength of Genevieve'character. She went to Margaret's store-room (which equates to her boyfriend's conscience, a store of feelings and emotions) and took some provisions as recompense (left him in no doubt as to the selfish side of his nature).

Incidentally, having read this interpretation several times, the subject might be surprised to realize how similar her boyfriend is to Margaret in certain aspects of their characters.

On her way home (out of the relationship with her boyfriend), Genevieve passed another grocery store (her own subconscious or conscience). It was then that she considered Margaret's ulterior motives. We know that Margaret was a political activist in real life and the dream elects to show this. In doing so, it is pointing to the side of Genevieve's boyfriend she dislikes and now under-stands. He was using her for his own gratification, and thought only of himself.

Finally, the reason behind the dream. It serves two purposes: first, it is showing the dreamer that she is not prepared to be put upon or taken for a ride, which is excellent, and should help her get over this relationship. Second, it is storing this experience in her memory, so that she will recognize this character trait in prospective suitors and avoid becoming entangled in any similar situation in the future.

✳ ✳ ✳

Genevieve told us: 'I was absolutely thrilled to receive your inter-pretation of my dream. Your analysis was very accurate.'

Now let us take a look at the dream from an astrological point of view. This was another fairly complex dream to analyse. However, by studying the symbols and also looking at the chart beforehand for any significant clues, the interpretation gradually came to light.

Astrological Interpretation

Genevieve has a Libra ascendant, with her Sun in Aries in the section of the chart related to partnerships, relationships and other people. This immediately tells us that she is continuously aware of other people and also of how they are seeing her. She is conscious of her image in their eyes.

The Libra ascendant shows that she likes to appear balanced and harmonious, to present a pleasing image. Her Sun in Aries in the seventh house signifies that she enjoys working with others, but at the same time likes to be in a leading position, or working independently within the group. She has a pioneering spirit.

Her Sun in Aries makes a challenging aspect to her natal Neptune in Libra situated in the section of the chart related to image, personality and self-expression. This reveals that there is an element of confusion in her relationships with others. They do not see Genevieve as she really is, and Genevieve herself sometimes confuses areas of her own personality with those of others. Neptune is a very diffuse and somewhat puzzling planet to deal with. It tends to erode the borders between one thing and another, or one personality and another, so that things under its influence can merge into an amorphous mass.

Genevieve's dream seems to allude to her own confusion and to her deception by her friend Margaret, which ties in with the above aspect. However, we will now take a closer look at the dream to find out what additional information the chart can supply.

Genevieve begins by telling us that in her dream her friend Margaret was selling her a word processor. This, a transaction involving a friend, immediately ties us into the seventh house, the section of the chart related to deals, contracts, partnerships and relationships.

If we start by looking at the house connected with friends, we find that Leo on the cusp reveals the Sun as its ruler, and the Sun is situated in Aries in the seventh house. So we are brought round full circle to the seventh house again.

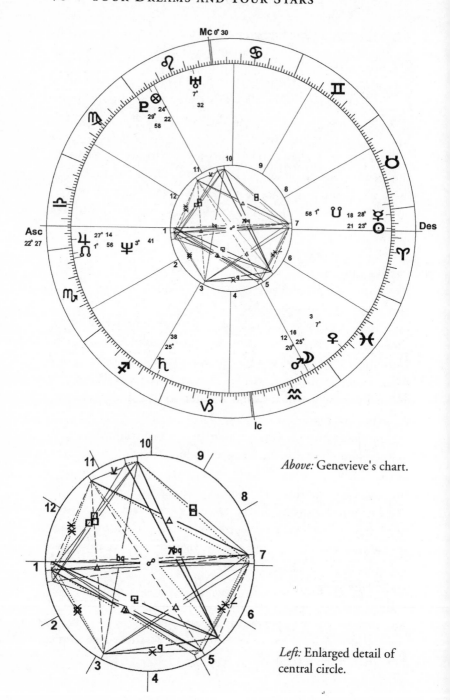

Above: Genevieve's chart.

Left: Enlarged detail of central circle.

As a word processor is a symbol for communication, it refers to the planet Mercury, which is situated in Taurus, in the section of the chart concerned with relationships, partnerships and other people. Mercury is also placed in opposition to Neptune, which can again imply confusion in communications with others: they just don't come out right, somehow.

Genevieve tells us that the agreed selling price (written in bold type) was £64, and that this was the amount of her child allowance and single-parent benefit. Anything to do with social security or state benefits comes under the influence of the eleventh house, which, as mentioned earlier, is governed by Leo and ruled by the Sun in Aries, in the section of the chart related to partnerships and relationships.

In Genevieve's chart, both Pluto and Jupiter are situated in the section concerning friends, groups, clubs and social welfare, and they are both in close proximity or conjunct. Both also aspect her natal Mercury and Sun, forming a harmonious angle, although they also present a challenging aspect to her Moon.

It seems, from looking further at Genevieve's chart, that she sees her friends, and to some extent the state system, as holding a lot of power. She may find herself quite enjoying the interaction between her friends and 'the system' as regards her rights as an individual, and her freedom as a person, yet also secretly mistrusting them.

She goes on to say that she wrote out a cheque for the correct amount, discovered that she had already paid Margaret for the computer, and proceeded to ask for the money back. This again reveals problems concerning Mercury, the planet of communication, which is in opposition to Neptune, the planet of confusion. Margaret did not tell Genevieve that she had already paid her for it, and Genevieve had forgotten. Deceit and confusion were involved in the transaction.

Genevieve threatened to call the police, and when Margaret still refused to pay her back, she dialled 999. The situation had now become a crisis, and this kind of event comes under the influence of the eighth house, which relates to change, transformation, crisis, things hidden from view, birth, death, etc. Genevieve's Moon is in Taurus in this section of the chart. The Moon quite often shows how we react to things when under pressure. Here, she reacted by calling the police.

She describes how 'a whole troop of policemen and women arrived' but there was nothing they could do. The fact that they could not help shows that it was futile for her to make a stand. She then considered taking Margaret to court.

Courts and the law are ruled by the ninth house, which relates to law, higher education, broadening horizons and travel. This section of Genevieve's chart is governed by the sign of Gemini and ruled by the planet Mercury, which, as we discovered earlier, is situated in the seventh house in opposition to Neptune, creating an energy of mental confusion and communication problems.

Genevieve decided against going to court as she felt that the judge would rule against her. This seems to indicate that she was not thinking straight. She was not putting the natural fairness and logic of the system to the test, but deciding, judging from her own value system, that she would lose.

Next, Genevieve found herself in Margaret's storeroom, where she took what she estimated to be about £7 worth of provisions as compensation for being cheated.

Possessions come under the influence of the second house which, in this instance, is ruled by Pluto (Scorpio, governed by Pluto, is on the cusp of the second house). This brings us back to the Pluto/Jupiter conjunction in the section of the chart related to friends, groups and the social system.

Saturn, the North Node and the Part of Fortune are also in this section of Genevieve's chart, which is connected to issues of self-worth as well as possessions. The North Node, in this section of the chart, indicates that she would benefit from looking at issues surrounding self-esteem and financial worth, particularly as Saturn is positioned here, highlighting her need to learn to value her many talents and achievements. Both the North Node and the Part of Fortune denote that she would make rapid strides forward if she could improve her self-esteem.

It seems as though, owing to her lack of self-esteem, Genevieve has allowed friends to take advantage of her in the past. She takes just £7 as compensation, which is a long way short of the £64 she is owed. However, one gets the impression that she did not feel she had any right to get this money back; she claimed back what she felt she was worth.

Pluto in the chart tends to represent areas where there are specific energy blocks. By releasing these blocks, we can quickly move forward, using the energy in a new and more life-enhancing way. Pluto in the social section of the chart shows that Genevieve has problems with peer groups and social set-ups, which are made more complex by a challenging aspect to her natal Moon, in the section of the chart connected with change, transformation, crisis and life alterations. This means that she may be inclined secretly to mistrust her friends, suspecting them of having ulterior motives, and feel unable completely to relax in their company.

This seems to be confirmed by Genevieve's suggestion that Margaret may have wanted the money for some political objective, and didn't care how she got it. She feels that her friends do not want to know her for herself, but because she has something that they want. This brings us back to the subject of self-worth. Genevieve needs to love and appreciate herself, and then to be able to feel that others also love and appreciate her for herself.

Looking at the dream in its entirety, it seems to be dealing with a number of issues concerning Genevieve's self-esteem and how she communicates with others. Both problems seem to create a kind of vicious circle: the more communications become muddled, the more she distrusts others, and the less she values herself, believing that others only wish to take advantage of her.

The image of the word processor appears to be quite important, as it relates to the planet Mercury, which symbolizes communication. It seems that Genevieve would benefit from trying to comprehend the true meaning of any communication, rather than assuming she has heard or understood.

If we now take a look at the transits that were in operation when she had the dream, we can see that Pluto was conjuncting her natal Saturn in the section of the chart connected with possessions, personal finances and issues of self-worth. Here, Pluto would be helping her to see the self-imposed barriers to her fulfilment. Pluto was also making an aspect to her natal Mercury in Taurus, showing that it is now time to re-examine the ways she communicates and uses her mind, the way she thinks.

Pluto transits nearly always coincide with dramatic, although slow-moving changes. Genevieve's subconscious mind was urging her to examine the issues discussed above. The dream spells out the nature of the problem, and over the year, as Pluto again aspects these points, she will be able to learn more and finally begin to value herself and her contribution to life.

In her progressions chart, the progressed Moon was also moving through Scorpio and through the section connected with possessions and self-worth. So it seems that the issue of self-esteem currently needs working on quite urgently, the issue of communication being equally significant.

Summary

Genevieve fears someone is taking advantage of her, but it is important that she looks deeply into all her relationships, to find out where the error actually lies. This is not to say that she should allow anyone to walk all over her, but that, by developing her self-esteem, she will automatically form the kind of friendships which are worthy of her and will support her, as she, in turn, can offer help and support.

The keys appear to be clarifying her boundaries, knowing when to say 'yes' and 'no' to the demands of others, valuing herself and improving her communications with others. All of these factors will help her to move on to a more secure, loving level of being.

Comparisons and Conclusions

In a final analysis of Genevieve's dream, let us consider the more positive aspects of combining both methods of interpretation. Highlighting different levels of meaning can give singularly helpful results in the case of enigmatic dreams.

The analytical approach can determine, to begin with, whether a given dream is a message-bearing one. This is most important, as some dreams may merely be processing the day's events, or fulfilling the dreamer's desires. They may also, for instance, be lucid, which means they cannot be interpreted because they have come under conscious control. Understanding the nature of the dreaming process itself enables a lot of false starts and misinterpretations to be excluded.

Not all dreams can readily be translated via the birth chart. The energies involved may be connected with certain potent astrological aspects, rather than with a particular house. As we shall see later in the book, they may not be based on the natal chart at all, but on a particular transit or progression currently in motion. However, it is definitely worth spending the time and trouble to find out if a dream can be linked to the horoscope, as the evidence in earlier chapters reveals.

In the case of Genevieve's dream, the link with the chart provided several clues to other facets of meaning. While on one level the dream confirmed her problems with her boyfriend, on another it also demonstrated that low self-esteem was the root cause of the difficulty in her relationship with him.

The chart furnishes information about the individual, which can aid and enrich the interpretation, showing whether they are, for example, practical, emotional, fiery, intellectual, or a blend of these. It also demonstrates where their main priorities lie.

This vital data is linked in with the dream, and the transits and progressions together put it into perspective. They also provide a time reference, indicating how long a period of change or unsettlement will last.

Genevieve's dream, and her relationship with her boyfriend, are signs that it may help her to work on her sense of self-esteem, and look at the way in which she communicates with others. Tackling both these issues would help to improve her relationships in the future.

We have established that the two systems of interpretation address different issues: the flow-chart method deals primarily with the dream itself, whereas the astrological interpretation focuses on the individual's personality in relationship to the dream. It is hardly surprising, then, if they seem to be dissimilar in places, but the systems are complementary and merge at the crux of the message.

We decided to include Genevieve's dream because it is our only case where, at first glance, there are considerable differences between the analyses. (The remaining interpretations in this book are stunningly similar.) We know from Genevieve's letter that she was thrilled with the flow-chart interpretation and the advice given by her own subconscious, but what did she think about the astrological analysis?

Full of curiosity, we sent Genevieve the second analysis and, with bated breath, awaited her comments. We were delighted when we received her reply, which, in itself, went a long way to validate our theories. Here is an extract from her letter:

> I did not waste any time continuing a relationship that was not going to work out. Had I have been less in touch with my intuition and my dreams, I might have done.
>
> However, there are myriad layers to dreams, and Helen Adams has accurately analysed other levels. I am being very open and honest when I admit that she is right about the self-esteem. Then she hit the nail on the head when she said that I don't trust groups.

Genevieve went on to reveal many aspects of her character which Helen's interpretation had identified. The fact that she could see instantly that both analyses were correct and centered on the same issues was very rewarding for us.

Several months later, curious to know whether Genevieve had acted on the analyses, we contacted her again. She reported that, in the main, she had been too busy getting on with life and her studies to give the matter a great deal of time and thought. Nevertheless, she added that, in view of the interpretations, she had made up her mind to communicate better with people and to project a more accurate image of herself, and had begun by studying two books on the subject of communication. She also told us that she was now more aware of the need to believe in herself and develop a greater degree of self-esteem.

CHAPTER 8

Turning-points

 n this chapter we will look at dreams that represent major turning-points and see how these reflect the qualities of both the ascendant/descendant axis and the *imum coeli*/midheaven (IC/MC) axis.

The Ascendant/Descendant Axis

The ascendant/descendant axis represents two highly significant points in the chart. The ascendant is the birth point of the horoscope. It divides everything pertaining to the subconscious, or what is as yet unmanifest, from all that is about to emerge into awareness, into full consciousness. Therefore, the ascendant is strongly related to new beginnings, to getting things going, and to the start of new cycles. It is also connected to the development of our personality and ego, and the emergence from a fragile state to that of a fully confident and self-expressive person.

Any planets situated close to the ascendant or in the first house of the chart affect our personalities in many ways. Someone with Saturn situated on the ascendant would have a far more serious way of expressing themselves than someone with Jupiter in the same place.

The following dream is a good illustration of the way in which this point in the chart is communicated through dreams. The dreamer was by the sea, on a beach divided in half by a border of rock running along its length. The wall of rock was solid except for a small gap. Standing by this gap, the dreamer suddenly noticed a tidal wave building up in the sea and moving at rapid speed towards the hole in the rock. She realized that she could very well be submerged by it and drown, but for some reason remained by the gap as the wave continued its course up the beach. She stood waiting as the tidal wave burst in full force through the gap and swirled around her entire body, cocooning and protecting her from its force. She remembers being relieved and very grateful to the powers above for this release from danger.

In her chart, this subject has a Cancer ascendant, which is naturally associated with the beach. It also means that the Moon is her ruling planet and that its potent effect on water, both on the surface of the planet and within the human body, would be a strong influence in her life, particularly through her emotions.

The wall of rock in her dream represents the actual line of the ascendant, dividing unconsciousness from consciousness. The gap represents the point of birth, where the unmanifest moves into manifestation.

The dreamer appears to be waiting on the borders of consciousness, half-expecting a message, an intuition, a movement of energy from the subconscious mind. She realized, in the dream, that something is coming from within the depths of herself, perhaps on a scale greater than she bargained for.

As she watched and the wave gathered strength, she wondered how she would cope with this huge torrent of energy, feeling small, frail and puny in comparison. When the wave struck and came arching through the gap, she felt a sense of surrender, as though there was nothing she could do; it didn't occur to her to run away. The wave then made a complete oval around her body and, as she said, seemed to be protecting her. The huge torrent of energy didn't overpower her; she remained safe, partly because of her attitude of surrender.

We feel the dream was telling her that, by persevering with her studies of meditation and the unconscious mind, she had released this energy from within: the energy of the self. By surrendering to it, she would help to bring this energy to birth, and in turn it would help bring her to birth.

The opposite pole, the descendant, concerns the line between our personal concerns and the concerns of others, the group, the community. It is the demarcation between selfhood and otherness. Quite often this point in the chart also represents what psychologists call the 'shadow' side of our nature, the parts of ourselves we intensely dislike and may project out on to others. Feelings of repulsion or even loathing for a person we meet may be aroused because they are acting out in front of us some of our own most despised and repressed behaviour patterns. It is also quite common for people to dislike a person because of a particular habit or character trait, one which they know their friends can see in them.

Astrologically, any sign in opposition to another usually contains elements which those born under its opposite sign would do well to try to develop.

In another dream, the dreamer was walking along (nowhere in particular) when she came across a female faun-type creature, with hairy legs and cloven feet. Dejected and bedraggled, it was standing behind a black iron-railing fence. Looking really fed up and more than a little angry with the dreamer, she said something like, 'Why don't you pay more attention to me?' The dreamer walked off feeling very guilty and not knowing what to do.

The sign of the descendant in her chart is Capricorn, which is ruled by Saturn and often connected with goats, but usually with the figure of Pan (who, in this Christianized era, is often associated with the devil). The dream seems to be saying that the dreamer is keeping a part of herself in bondage and not allowing it its rightful expression, blatantly ignoring it, in fact.

The shadow is this case is represented by Capricornian traits, which include strong down-to-earth and practical characteristics, as well as a keen sense of ambition, the need to achieve goals, despite the hard work this entails. Capricorns often display a strong financial sense, which others may interpret as gross materialism, but which in its highest sense is an understanding of the nature of money.

The dream is suggesting to the dreamer that she should not ignore these earthier instincts, but pay attention to the practical concerns of life, which are essential, although they may at times seem boring.

As Capricorn is also ruled by the planet Saturn, the dreamer may well need to look at how she is using the Saturnian energy in her life, to what degree she is incorporating it into her everday world. If she expresses the Capricornian side of her nature, she will find that those problems relating to a misunderstanding and misuse of this energy will gradually resolve.

The IC/MC Axis

The IC/MC axis represents our path through life, and reveals both our roots and the soil in which we thrive, as well as our way forward in life and our public image. This axis is very often related to changes in the life path, especially when aspected by the transpersonal planets (Uranus, Neptune and Pluto).

Another dream from our files, which happened at a significant time in the dreamer's life, was connected with this particular axis. The subject dreamed she was living in the country, in a house on the edge of a wood. Next to the house was a stable, which she entered. The stable was dark, and had been totally cleaned out; there was no trace of straw or dung anywhere. However, there was a sense of expectancy, as though a major event, such as a birth, was about to occur. There was a dirt floor, and on another level a raised platform built of black stone which was very shiny. Some of the stones had deep score marks in them. On the top of this plat-form there were a few pebbles. The dreamer picked up one of the pebbles and it fell into two halves in her hand, to reveal a small, black, intricately-carved statue of a bearded man dressed in robes, sitting in contemplation. She felt overjoyed at this discovery.

In keying this dream into the chart, we connected the theme of birth (the feeling that something had been gestating) and the colour black to the planet Pluto, which was conjunct the IC.

Pluto is very much linked with the change and transformation of old energies which now serve no life-enhancing purpose, and are in fact holding the person back; the old way of functioning needs to end so that the energy can be used more usefully. Pluto also features strongly in predictions of birth, on a variety of levels.

When Pluto is conjunct the IC, it suggests that elements from the person's genetic make-up or behavioural patterns passed on down the family line may be causing problems or blockages in their life. Pluto was squaring itself in the dreamer's chart at the time, which suggested that there was a way for her to acknowledge and understand these processes and bring them to a successful conclusion by clearing them out and introducing more applicable ones.

At about this time, the dreamer was making great progress in her understanding of shamanism and the shamanic world, a path which understands and endorses the need to clear the ancestral blood line of damaging patterns.

Acting on the message of the dream made a significant difference to the way the dreamer feels about herself, and her continued commitment to the shamanic way also had a profound effect on her life path.

The dream contained further clues to the way her shamanic path would develop. The tiny man in the pebble represented the philosopher's stone, the supreme goal of alchemists, and signified the search for understanding and discovery of the higher self. It implied that the shamanic path would lead the dreamer to seek a higher understanding, a process that would be brought to fruition with the help of her inner teacher.

The equal house system

One practice in astrology, the house system, directly affects dream interpretation involving the angles. There are two basic types: the equal house system, and the methods based on the quadrant system. We shall not go into the different systems in detail, or argue for one over another, but, having interpreted charts using a variety of systems, we find that the equal house system consistently gives the best results in natal and predictive work.

Using the quadrant system, the IC/MC axis always becomes the cusp of the fourth and tenth houses. We find the equal house system more reliable in that the IC/MC can fall in the second, third, fourth or fifth house. This gives a guide from which the ancestral patterns and the path ahead can be traced.

Some families have specific values or long-established patterns connected with resources, echoing the second and eighth house polarity. Others may have an academic background, linked to the third/ninth polarity, others again a more karmic and predestined role, echoing the fourth and tenth polarity, or a creative role, as in the fifth/eleventh polarity.

This information is highly useful in dream interpretation because it provides vital background information showing where the client is literally coming from and going to. Thus dreams related to the angles take on a more personalized meaning.

Two short dreams from our files suggest a link with the MC, or midheaven point of the chart, as it is commonly known. In the first dream, the dreamer (a woman) finds herself in a public place, like the outside of a shopping mall, full of people milling about. She looks down to see that she is wearing nothing but her underwear. People come and talk to her and she finds she has to go and buy something; all the time she is acutely aware of being naked.

In this particular person's chart the midheaven is in the eighth house (using the equal house method). This house connects with change, irrevocable transformation, deep emotions and bonds, the hidden side of life, other people's finances or resources, and power issues. The midheaven is also in the sign of Aquarius, conjunct Venus and in opposition to Pluto.

The midheaven coincides with our public image, and it is clear from the dream alone that the dreamer feels very vulnerable, virtually naked, in public. Developing some kind of image or an awareness of the roles we all play would help this person to cope more efficiently in a public role.

The aspects involved with the midheaven indicate that deep emotions surround her value systems and resources and her need to project the right image. This suggests that the dreamer often feels exposed, as though wearing her heart on her sleeve. Venus in Aquarius indicates that she tries to maintain a cool exterior in order to hide the strong feelings which she is always fighting to control.

In the next dream, the same dreamer is again almost naked in a public place, but this time she is quite happy about it and doesn't feel at all worried. She continues to interact as though nothing is wrong and feels quite relaxed.

This dream took place after a transit of Pluto to its own natal place, squaring Venus and the IC/MC axis at virtually the same time. This reveals that emotions have been cleared out and sorted through, and the dreamer is much happier about them and her path through life. Consequently she feels more at ease in the public eye. Even though she is exposed, she is at peace with herself.

Dreams like these, supported by transits to the various angles of the chart, can herald psychological changes, especially when there is a recurrent theme connected to a particular angle of the chart. Any transits aspecting the angles, particularly the transpersonal planets (Uranus, Neptune and Pluto), will have a far-reaching effect on the subject's way of life, which is why these dreams can be such vital clues as to how we are progressing, or maybe holding ourselves back.

By keeping a dream log or dream diary we can begin to find definite links between our dreams, our natal and progressed charts and the accompanying transits. (An example of a personal dream report form is included on page 122.) Perhaps the most striking phenomenon of dreams is their creative use of images. Time and time again the subconscious produces astonishingly apt images relating to specific astrological placements. A written record will aid our understanding the relationship of these images to our individual energy pattern and keep us informed about our personal and spiritual progress.

CHAPTER 9

Spiritual Dreams

owadays our mail-bag produces an ever-increasing number of reports of dreams which, when analysed, are found to be spiritual in nature, or to contain elements of spirituality. Interestingly, this increase has also coincided with the general trend towards separation into distinct social and religious categories, with ever more entrenched attitudes and beliefs.

It may be that the established churches have failed to keep up with modern trends and no longer satisfy our spiritual needs. Today it seems easier than ever before to adopt new and radical philosophies. As we approach the millenium, spiritualism, occult sects, paganism and 'New Age' alternative beliefs are gaining in popularity. Some people claim that this move away from conventional Christianity is a symptom of a new understanding that is simmering beneath the surface, to emerge at the dawn of a new age of spirituality.

Spiritual dreams appear in a variety of guises, from the clear-cut to the obscure or outlandish. They may incorporate obviously spiritual symbols, such as a church, priest or crucifix. One client reported a dream in which he was kneeling in front of an archbishop, who was lit from behind by a bright light. The presence of an altar rail and other religious artefacts in the dream setting left little doubt as to the category into which the dream fell.

Slightly more obscure spiritual dreams feature the dreamer's relatives or friends who have died. These dreams offer reassurance, issue a warning or, more usually, convey a symbolic message of encouragement.

One such dream which we encountered involved the dreamer's deceased father, who appeared standing in the shadows, leaning on a walking stick and, uncharacteristically, wearing a smart dark grey suit and trilby hat. He apologized for speaking in an American accent (foreign languages or accents in dreams sometimes indicate a spiritual realm). Before he departed, the dreamer noticed a sort of mist swirling around her father's head, as though he literally had his head in the clouds.

The dream translated into an interpretation suggesting that the dreamer – in waking life – had been placing far too much emphasis on material values (symbolized by the dark grey suit) and on her appearance, to the detriment of her spiritual development (the mist).

Some spiritual dreams take place in bizarre settings or are accompanied by fantastic visual imagery. In one instance, the dreamer found herself in a primitive environment, surrounded by brutal-looking warriors engaged in bloody combat. Whenever a warrior was killed, the dreamer saw the body go up in a puff of mist and float away.

The dream was interpreted as a reflection of the futility of war. As a result of the analysis, the client took an active role in aid work to assist various war-ravaged countries.

Such dreams usually point to ways in which the dreamer can advance their spirituality, by positive action, meditative contemplation, or a combination of both. Sometimes the dreams serve to provide comfort and reassurance and give a boost to the subject's confidence.

Dreams of reincarnation

Some dreams which recur offer glimpses of the subjects' past lives. It is these dreams in particular which are becoming more and more frequent: it seems that reincarnation is not prepared to wait to be verified, but is thrusting itself with some urgency into the conscious mind.

David's research has identified three consistent elements in these dreams:

1. They are accompanied by strong emotions.
2. The dreamers do not recognize their own bodies.
3. The clothes in these dreams do not date from the present and are often from a much earlier period.

Dr Brian Weiss, author of *Only Love is Real*, reported a dream which he claimed reflected a past life; it contained all these three elements, as did Jenny Cockell's dream, described in detail in her fascinating book *Yesterday's Children*. In addition, Dr Hearne has found that these same elements are often present in experiences of past-life regression.

In the next chapter, we move on to describe another recurring theme that sometimes indicates a spiritual dream. It must be emphasized, however, that this is not the only possible interpretation of such dreams.

CHAPTER 10

Elizabeth's Dream

Elizabeth, the subject of the dream studied in this chapter, suffers from advanced multiple sclerosis. Almost totally paralysed and unable to write, she dictates her dreams to her mother who, in turn, sends them to David for analysis. He has interpreted several of Elizabeth's dreams and learned a great deal from them.

Elizabeth, as her dreams have revealed, is very spiritually advanced. Full of love, she bears no anger about her devastating illness and wonders if it might be a result of her karma. She has a high IQ, is proficient in many foreign tongues and, before her dread disease took hold, taught herself how to play the piano, mastering many of the classics.

When a subject dreams of being in a foreign country and there is some confusion as to which country it is, sometimes this indicates a spiritual realm. Elizabeth has dreamed of being lost in a foreign country, and about maps of a country that actually represent a neighbouring land. She has also experienced a 'flash sequence', suddenly finding herself in a different country.

Another recurring theme in Elizabeth's and other subjects' spiritual dreams is a confusion between left and right. This phenomenon indicates a possible confusion (in waking life) as to which side of the brain is predominantly used with regard to matters of spirituality.

Within a short period of time, David interpreted three dreams for Elizabeth and one for Gaynor Davies, fiction editor of *Woman's Weekly* magazine (see also *Dream Interpretation – The Secret*). He was amazed by the remarkable similarity of these four dreams, which contained several identical elements and were most definitely spiritual in nature.

The following dream, as yet unpublished, is the last of the three dreams sent in by Elizabeth for analysis.

SUBJECT:
✳ Elizabeth G.
✳ British
✳ Born 2.30 am,
31 August 1949
✳ Artist and musician
✳ Introvert

The Dream

✳ *I was driving in England, then in a flash, I was driving in the US. I was on the left-hand side of a very busy road with three lanes each way, but I felt completely safe.* ✳

Flow-chart Interpretation

Again, we have a spiritual dream. Elizabeth was driving in England and, in a flash, found herself driving in the US. The fact that she was driving on the left is extremely relevant to the previous two dreams, which we now know were indicating her lack of spiritual confidence. Astonishingly, this dream is almost a replica of that reported by Gaynor Davies: she, too, was driving on the wrong side of the road, and there was confusion as to exactly which country she was in.

Like Gaynor's dream, this one indicates that, for a while, Elizabeth was considering matters of spirituality from the wrong perspective. She was using the left side of her brain, the side that pertains to calculating logic, so it is little wonder that, although she knew she was on the wrong side of the road, she felt safe: because she was using the left brain, she remained detached, at a safe distance.

The dream was telling her that, in order to continue her journey of spiritual development, Elizabeth would have to think with her heart and employ the right side of her brain, the side related to creativity, spontaneity, inspiration and emotion.

✳ ✳ ✳

Although this was a relatively short dream with a brief interpretation, for Elizabeth it carried a poignant message, and one which made a lot of sense.

Astrological Interpretation

Elizabeth has a Cancer ascendant, which shows that on a first-impressions basis she comes across as being very friendly and highly sensitive to the feelings and emotions of other people. She is able to sense the emotions of others even though they may be trying to hide them from her.

This sensitivity of her Cancer ascendant combined with her Pisces midheaven means that she is tuned in to moods and feelings, and the fact that she is an artist and musician reflects this ability to express subtle feeling tones.

Her Sun is conjunct Saturn in the section of the chart related to personal possessions, values and feelings of self-worth. This combination of planets shows a tremendous discipline and the ability to master difficult and complex subjects which require dexterity and skill.

The section of Elizabeth's chart which relates to the nervous system is the third house, which in her case is connected to the sign Virgo and is ruled by the planet Mercury. Both Virgo and Mercury have very strong connections to the way our nervous system functions, often revealing whether we tend to live on our nerves or are able to relax. It seems Saturn's return to its own place in Virgo corresponded to the early years of this disease.

Elizabeth's feeling that contracting MS is perhaps some kind of karma may be reflected by the fact that Saturn, the planet of limitation and karma, is conjunct her Sun, the implication being that she may have elected to pay off what she feels is a karmic debt.

Having to deal with such suffering on a daily basis would tend to connect Elizabeth to a spiritual realm and so it is not surprising that this is represented in her dreams.

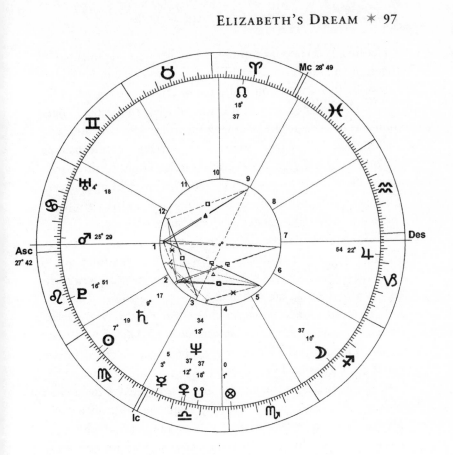

Above: Elizabeth's chart.

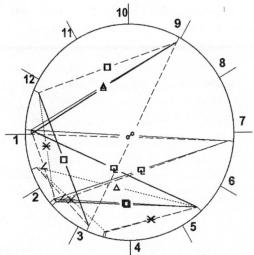

Right: Enlarged detail
of central circle.

Her dream corresponds to the axis in her chart represented by the third and ninth houses, which are opposite each other. This is shown by the fact that she is driving in England, a place familiar to her. This relates to the third house, which is connected to one's local area or familiar places, driving and other skills, and also communication, the nervous system and the exchange of information.

The rest of the dream concerns a foreign country; this comes under the ninth house, which is concerned with overseas travel, foreign countries, beliefs, higher education and the ability to move into new realms of experience or states of being.

The general background to the dream is the sudden switch from driving (i.e. functioning) in a well-known environment, to being in completely different surroundings (the US), new territory, where the rules are different.

As the ninth house concerns the bigger picture, and a more holistic view than that of the third house, the US – The *United States* – may symbolize a place where life is experienced at a more holistic, all-inclusive level.

In Elizabeth's chart the ninth house is connected with the sign of Pisces, which in turn is ruled by Neptune. Both Pisces and Neptune are concerned with the essence of oneness which underlies the whole of human experience, the sense of mystical unity often spoken about by saints and yogis. The attainment of this state helps to overcome the perception that all people and things are separate and distinct from each other.

However, Neptune is situated in the third house, the one related to detail, to the familiar, to skills needed in connection with everyday life, such as driving and reading. Neptune is also conjunct Venus, the planet which relates to the symbolism of emotional relationships. Both Neptune and Venus are in Libra, the sign of the scales. The area where Libra is situated in the chart is the one in which we are symbolically trying to find a state of balance. Here we find Neptune, which tends to blend issues, in the section of the chart where, for the sake of communication, they need to be clearly defined.

This suggests that Elizabeth's perception of everyday reality is not quite in focus, or that she is using her capacity to blend and fuse ideas rather inappropriately. It might be advisable for her to use the blending and refining qualities of Neptune to understand other states of consciousness, to reach the metaphorical United States, rather than for functioning in daily life.

In her dream, Elizabeth finds herself on the left-hand side of the busy road, with three lanes of traffic going each way, yet she feels safe. Despite the rapid transition to the 'United States', or the spiritual realm, she is coping very well there.

In the USA motorways like the one in Elizabeth's dream are called 'freeways', and we feel that the dream is pointing to a way of being free in the 'United States'. Using the spiritual qualities and refined emotions within to focus on other states of being, takes her out of her everyday environment and transports her to a spiritual dimension, where she may feel less restricted by her illness and suffering.

The dream could be urging her to try to move into other states by meditating, even if this is difficult for her. It could also be saying that if she makes an effort in this direction, she may suddenly find that she reaches a new state quite easily.

This idea is supported by the position of the North and South Nodes in Elizabeth's chart. These indicate qualities we should develop in this lifetime, and the areas where we concentrate too much energy. In Elizabeth's chart the North Node is in Aries, in the section of the chart related to long-distance travel and opening up to new experiences. This suggests that she should adopt a pioneering attitude and not be afraid to venture into unknown realms. The position of the South Node indicates that she should pay less attention to the mundane, trivial details of her life.

Although no exact date is given for Liz's dream, it happened within the first two weeks of September 1995. The chart progressions for this period reveal that her progressed Moon was moving through the sign of Leo and the section of her chart related to new beginnings, new chapters in the book of life.

As far as the transits are concerned, Jupiter, the planet of expansion and freedom, was making a challenging square aspect to her natal Sun conjunct Saturn in Virgo. Jupiter represents the urge for freedom from restricting conditions. At the time of Elizabeth's dream, it was moving through the sign of Sagittarius, which is ruled by Jupiter and relates to a similar desire to transcend boundaries and move into new realms of experience.

The natal Sun conjunct Saturn in Virgo suggests restricted living conditions. The sign of Virgo is quite often identified with the body and bodily functions, particularly the way in which the mind and body interact to produce our perceived reality. This also applies to the daily routine of our habits, thoughts and actions, which contribute to our reality.

So here the principle of freedom, of moving into new territory (to other countries or mental states), is in conflict with the limited reality of the body and the daily routine connected with it. This transit ties in with the dream's message about finding a way to move beyond the body and its suffering by focusing on a higher, more holistic state of being.

Comparisons and Conclusions

Linking Elizabeth's dream with her natal chart revealed much of interest, especially concerning the right- and left-brain functions. Both the dream and the chart, as well as the two interpretations, drew attention to Elizabeth's left-brain approach to spirituality.

The third house of the chart, ruled by Mercury, is connected with using the mind in the more logical or left-brain mode. However, the ninth house of the chart is also connected with the use of the mind for higher understanding, emphasizing the value of intuition, which is linked to the right brain.

Elizabeth's subconscious used the idea of the 'United States' to indicate the higher, holistic level of consciousness experienced by saints and mystics, which would come under the influence of the ninth and twelfth houses of the chart. To emphasize this issue even more, in Elizabeth's chart Gemini is on the cusp of the mystical twelfth house and Sagittarius is on the cusp of the highly organized and analytical sixth house. Once again, this reveals that she may benefit from a change in outlook (adopting a more right-brain approach).

The flow-chart analysis and the astrological interpretation agree that the switch from one country to another in the dream concerns spiritual matters and the way in which they are approached. This seems particularly appropriate, because a move to a more holistic state of consciousness might ease her difficult daily life.

In general, to ascertain other signs of spirituality in the chart, one would need to look at the position of Jupiter and Neptune, the signs of Pisces and Sagittarius, and the house cusps with which they equate, as well as the situation of the ninth and twelfth houses. It is not possible to determine someone's level of spiritual awareness by looking at the chart alone, only their potential development.

Some people have exceptionally complicated charts, with many squares, oppositions and difficult conjunctions, yet they seem to thrive despite their problems. Others have charts replete with trines and harmonious conjunctions, but are lazy and miserable.

Our dreams are very good guide to our actual state of consciousness. We may be able to fool others, and we may fool ourselves, but if we work with our dreams we will not be content to pretend we are saintly and highly evolved beings, especially when we have glimpsed our shadow side. The study of our dreams and our charts provides a reliable method of understanding the truth about ourselves.

Elizabeth's life offers little or no opportunity to act on the dream's apparent message that she should meditate. From dawn till dusk she has to endure many disturbances, which make silent contemplation almost impossible.

Nevertheless, spiritually, she is already very advanced and accepts her illness without anger. As we have seen, she believes that it might be the result of a karmic debt, in which case the trials and tribulations of this life give her the opportunity to repay that debt and to make further spiritual progress.

Therefore, it seems likely that this is a dream of reassurance, too. The fact that it demanded a spiritual interpretation in itself served to comfort Elizabeth: she now feels that she is not alone, but is being watched over. The message of the dream bolstered her belief that following her heart, rather than employing too much left-brain, structured thinking, has a positive effect on how she copes with her ongoing ordeal.

CHAPTER 11

Archetypes

eep within the psyche of each individual, in the subconscious mind, there exist certain forces or energies which work as pre-set patterns, the antecedents of various experiences in that person's life. Carl Jung called these energies 'archetypes'.

Some examples of the more common archetypes or patterns are the mother, the father, birth, death and falling in love. A more complex one is that of the self, an integrated structure which embraces all aspects of the personality, including the ego. The self is a pattern of wholeness (but not necessarily of perfection) and strives to bring us into balance.

Many astrologers would agree that an individual's birth chart reveals their pre-set patterns and experience of these inner factors, and thus provides a way of understanding the underlying cause of dramas in their external life.

Let us consider the archetype of the mother, for example. Everyone has a mother, but for each individual, the image of the mother has a different connotation, which may be positive, negative, or, more often than not, a mixture of the two. In the birth chart the individual's perception of the mother is usually shown by the placement of the Moon, by sign, rulership, house and aspect. For instance, a person with the Moon in Taurus, in the fourth or domestic section of the chart, will probably have a vastly different perception of the mother archetype from someone with the Moon in Capricorn, in the second house of the chart.

To some extent we all project on to our real mother our mother archetype or pattern; she may or may not be aware of this.

When we are unaware of the presence and purpose of these energies, they will affect our environment, sometimes causing problems in our lives. For example, someone who has Uranus in the second house of the chart, which is connected with personal possessions, finances, values and self-esteem, will probably have a strong principles that may lead them to criticize the shallowness of outworn value systems and materialistic attitudes.

If such a person is unaware of this energy, they may suffer disaster upon disaster with their money and property until they learn to handle this area of life in a new way. This may involve adopting a radically different method of dealing with possessions, and learning to understand and follow their unique path in life. (The social norm of a regular earning pattern would probably be inappropriate in their case.) By doing so, they will tap into their own natural state of abundance.

Our dreams can give us many clues about which of our patterns or archetypes are in need of energy and attention. They must first be linked to the planets, signs and houses of the astrological chart, all of which are connected to similar themes, but represent different energy levels. For example, the first house of the chart has a similar vibration to the planet Mars and the sign of Aries, and the second is allied to Venus and the sign of Taurus. The planet represents the active force itself, the sign the way the force expresses itself and the house the area of life in which it is expressed.

The different aspects are like conversations, or the lack of communication, between the different patterns of energy, and this interaction contributes to the level of harmony in our lives.

As the planetary energies are the active components in the chart, we will now examine the archetypes or patterns of energy which they symbolize. This will show how the actions or dramas taking place in a significant dream can be traced back to them.

The Sun

The Sun encompasses the entire psyche, and its function as the higher or healing self is to bring all parts of the self, including the ego, to wholeness and integration, so that they can reach their full potential.

Our lives tend to function better when we listen to the guidance of our higher selves, and follow through with appropriate action. We become more self-confident and self-sufficient and have a strong sense of purpose. Sun energy brings a feeling of generosity, dignity, self-esteem and self-assurance. We are more creative and conscientious, and exhibit good leadership skills. We are, to use the modern description of an integrated personality, 'together'.

If the Sun energy is not functioning properly, we tend to see the world through the distorted lens of the ego, which can lead to self-centredness, general incompetence, destructiveness, a weak will and lack of purpose. This means that other elements of the chart can usurp the place of the Sun, and we may become unbalanced or lack focus in our lives.

A dream about losing a gold ring could well indicate the loss of the dreamer's unifying centre of being and of their purpose, gold being connected with the Sun and with the sign of Leo. A study of the dreamer's chart would reveal the particular complex of energies to which the dream was referring.

The Moon

The Moon in the birth chart represents the development of potential into actuality through the processes of gestation, birth, growth and death. The Moon brings plans, projects and ideas to fruition. Its influence is reactive and perceptive. Its effect in our charts relates to our experience of bringing things to birth, of our mothers, and mothering, of nurturing and how we meet our needs. When the Moon is functioning favourably in the chart, we are sensitive to the environment and to others and have a strong sense of creativity. We are also endowed with a fertile imagination, the ability to be receptive to life, a keen sense of intuition and a flair for productivity.

When it is not working so efficiently, we may become cut off from our own natural needs and rhythms. Our ability to care for ourselves is limited, and we have difficulty in realizing that others, too, require emotional support and nurturing. We may react over-sensitively to others and to the environment, and become fearful. We may also become unstable, because of a poor understanding of the timing of things, of allowing them to take root and grow naturally. Other potential problems are restlessness, fussiness and general apathy.

One woman dreamed that she travelled to the moon, and on the dark side met a man whom she described as 'a snivelling wimp'. The dream seemed to indicate that her inner male or animus needed to be strengthened so that he could support her in meeting her own needs and standing up for herself.

Mercury

Mercury represents the archetypal pattern of communication, of bridging gaps and making connections (hence its link with the nervous system). When it is functioning positively in the chart, adaptation to the environment flows smoothly, communication is effortless, and it is possible to convey and receive messages with very little difficulty. Studies go smoothly, aided by a good memory, and social skills are well developed.

When Mercury is not working so well in the chart, due to patterns which create negative thinking, blockages or feelings of inadequacy in this area, communication may originate from a negative standpoint and become defensive. There may be nervous tension, great restlessness and an inability to concentrate on one thing for long. Problems with the nervous system could cause tension and over-anxiety. The person concerned may become a gossip and be very cunning and manipulative. This kind of energy will naturally create associated problems in the environment.

Sometimes we dream that we are communicating in a way which is not our normal pattern of behaviour. One man dreamed that he was having a raging argument with a friend, which involved a lot of subtle word-play and innuendo. He awoke feeling really good about this as in reality he was very shy and retiring, never displayed anger, and was not a witty person, although he knew he had this ability within him.

It transpired that Jupiter was transiting his natal Mercury at the time of the dream, which may have been encouraging him to give a fuller expression to his moods and feelings.

Venus

Venus represents the ability to relate to others, to communicate and share emotions, rather than ideas, which come under the influence of Mercury. It embodies the capacity to harmonize and co-operate, to blend in, to create a shared atmosphere of constructive feeling. When Venus is functioning well in the chart, our relationships with others flow smoothly, with little friction. A point of balance is sought in any disagreement, so that both sides can gain something positive from the interaction. There is an understanding of how to create harmony in the environment, and an artistic streak which may manifest in a variety of ways.

When Venus is not functioning so well, many problems could arise in our relationships, because our ability to express our true feeling is thwarted. This could result in cold relationships in which duty becomes more important than genuine feeling, or, in severe cases, an absence of any sort of relationship. There may be a tendency towards over-indulgence, immorality, sloppiness and a lack of tact.

Dreams concerning relationships often link with Venus, the seventh house or Libra. One woman dreamed that she was just about to get married in a church, and was already wearing her wedding dress. At this point in the dream she was given a puzzle ring and told that the marriage would not be complete until she had worked out the puzzle and connected the separate segments, making the ring into one whole unit. Then she awoke.

Linking this dream into her natal chart would help distinguish the different elements of this dreamer's relationship 'puzzle', and harmonizing them would help her become whole, and able to attract harmonious relationships.

Mars

Mars, the next planetary principle, represents the archetype of energy and movement, action, getting things done and putting ideas into practice. It also stands for a degree of mastery over situations and the environment, such as taking control rather than letting things just drift.

When Mars is functioning well in the chart, we are naturally self-assertive without being dictatorial, have the capacity to get things done, a sense of courage and a willingness to compete in order to better ourselves. We will have an urge to move in new directions, to be pioneering, ambitious and enterprising.

When Mars is not functioning so well, the outcome is often reckless behaviour, a devil-may-care attitude and aggression expressed through rudeness. We may become quarrelsome and generally uncooperative, procrastinate, and have feelings of lust rather than love.

If someone dreamed of doing something daring, which required great skill and courage, the analyst might look at Mars in their natal chart to find out what message their subconscious was trying to convey.

Jupiter

Jupiter represents the principle of expansion, and of extending oneself out into the world. It promotes the mature handling of resources and the ability to communicate with others in order to expand possibilities and take up opportunities. Another function is to increase one's well-being and happiness through material, spiritual and mental gain, from study, trading, religious or other practices based on moral principles.

When Jupiter is working well in the chart, action flows in a way which is conducive to progress and general growth. We look towards the future with optimism, want to advance, and have consideration for other people. We are sociable, generous and just, and have a principled approach to and enjoyment of life. We are also trustworthy, hospitable, and have a natural buoyancy.

When Jupiter is 'afflicted', as older astrological texts put it, or in more modern phraseology, 'cosmically challenged', there will be problems with the aspects described above. There could be trouble with the law, difficulties with education, particularly with higher education. We may make promises which prove impossible to keep, over-extend time, energy and money, become over-indulgent and extravagant, and have a tendency to be too opinionated and self-seeking.

A business man dreamed that he was looking at himself in the mirror, and his image seemed to get bigger and bigger, rather like a balloon inflating. It became so big that he thought it would burst. As one quality of Jupiter is expansion, looking at the position of this planet by house, sign and aspect in the natal chart would perhaps throw some light on the interpretation.

Saturn

Saturn represents the principle of control and limitation; it corresponds to the skeletal structure in the body and to the limits we have to adopt in order to get things accomplished, or to prevent a state of constant chaos. Saturn equates with time and the constructive use of time. When we are using the Saturn principle effectively, we are good at managing our time and know how to discipline ourselves in order to get things done.

Other attributes of a positive Saturn expression are good relationships with people in authority and with the father. There is also the ability to work hard in difficult circumstances, in order to reach a clearly defined goal or ambition, or to overcome a particular difficulty.

When Saturn is not functioning well, there tend to be problems with the bones, or arthritic-type conditions. Our relationships with authority figures may become strained and troubled, and we may find ourselves frequently on the run from those in control. We may perceive an almost devilish quality in those in positions of power, including the father, feeling that they are out to get us. This is because we have projected Saturn, the archetype of discipline, on to these people, so that they seem oppressive or even tyrannical.

There may also be strong feelings of inadequacy in the sector in which Saturn is present, or if Saturn is aspecting another planet very closely. This would make it difficult for us to relax and be ourselves in circumstances represented by Saturn; we may have a tendency to try too hard in such situations.

The dreams in which we come face to face with aspects of our shadow side can often be linked to Saturn in the natal chart, as can those dreams in which we are very constricted and cramped.

For example, one dreamer found himself in his father's car (one of those old-fashioned open-topped models). In the dream he was far too big for the car and his knees were sticking out up above the windscreen. He became so squashed that he could not breathe properly. Aspects to Saturn, its placement and rulership in the dreamer's chart would be studied, and probably reveal much of interest concerning his relationship with his father.

Uranus

As a planetary principle, Uranus represents the archetype of sudden inspiration, new ideas, revolution, inventiveness and the kind of event which suddenly catapults one out of a routine situation into a new and more fulfilling way of life.

When Uranus is functioning well, people under the planet's influence possess a strong sense of individuality and individual purpose. They recognize their own unique talents and are not afraid to use them. Socially minded, they are eager to advance society by developing new methods and systems to improve life for everybody. They understand the nature of change and the need to incorporate the best of the old into a new framework.

When Uranus is functioning less well, we tend to be very self-centered and will stick to our own ideas in a stubborn and self-defeating way, determined not to fit in with others but to stand out for the sake of being different. We are inclined to be revolutionary in the sense of sweeping away the old completely

without considering how, or by what, it is to be replaced. We are
liable to force change for its own sake and quite often seem
unable to put down roots. We continually create upheaval in our
lives and suffer from a lack of continuity.

Uranus, like Neptune and Pluto, is regarded as a 'transpersonal'
planet, which means that its effect is beyond the control of the
ego. Dreams which come under its influence often seem to have
a profound message. One woman dreamed that she was in a huge
aircraft hangar (Uranus is often associated with aeroplanes, especially the technologically advanced types). A small but highly
powered plane, rather like a jet fighter, was parked there. Out
jumped a woman who was obviously the pilot. When the
dreamer asked her how she had managed to get such a good job,
she replied, 'I had to learn music.'

The dreamer felt that this dream contained an important message about learning to listen to her heart and to the promptings
of her inner self, even if these differed from society's expectations.
Again, linking this dream into the subject's chart would probably
provide clues about her deeper purpose in life.

Neptune

Neptune energy relates to blending and fusing things together,
blurring differences, so that energies merge and become one
rather than distinct from each other. As an archetypal process,
Neptune represents the understanding and realization of subtle
reality, of the one energy permeating the whole of creation.

People who are using Neptunian energy in a positive way tend
to be mystical, spiritual and psychic. They have a clear comprehension of the other levels of reality and can move between
dimensions. They see clearly and do not confuse or mix up their
information. They also gain a good deal of inspiration from the
higher levels. Artists, poets, musicians and dancers are quite often
tuned into the energy and ideas available from other realms.

Those whose Neptunian energy is not functioning so well are
apt to be deceived, or to deceive others. They seem to be in a per-

manent fog, not knowing where to go or what to do next. Quite often, they are taken advantage of by people stronger than themselves, caught up in relationships in which they assign themselves the role of victim. As victims, they can be despotic, constantly monopolizing the limelight with their problems and making others feel guilty when their needs are not met. They may also be prone to addictions or substance abuse.

The dream concerning the message from the man in the shoe shop about 'the ones that try to drain you' (see page 61) would link into Neptune. It illustrates the problem of being unable to say 'no', or create firm boundaries in life, which tends to leave one open to exploitation.

Pluto

Lastly, Pluto represents the principle of transformation and the removal of those elements and energies in one's life which are obstructing forward growth to make way for new, life-enhancing activities.

When Pluto is functioning well in the chart, there is a natural comprehension of the need for elimination: the need to clear the decks of old unwanted rubbish and conclude unfinished business. We accept that the end of one phase heralds the beginning of a new phase in life, and realize that birth and death are two sides of the same coin.

We also understand power and the use of power, not in the sense of rigid control, but in knowing when to hold on to something and when to let it go. This includes an understanding of shared resources and the principle of letting goods and money circulate, rather than hoarding them so that fresh supplies are prevented from coming in.

When Pluto is not functioning so well in the chart, there can be illnesses and other emotional or mental problems, caused by holding on to experiences from the past through an inability to let them go or to forgive and forget. This emotional clinging may result in instability, temper tantrums and depression, and stop any positive growth in our lives. The emotional repression, if unrelieved, will eventually give way to a massive explosion which could obliterate both good and bad together. It is better, it seems, to clear up as you go along, thus causing less stress all round.

Dreams which link into Pluto, Scorpio or the eighth house of the chart point to areas of our lives where change or transformation is required. One man dreamed that he was in a dark cave surrounded by poisonous black scorpions which were all poised to strike, tails arched. Feeling that something had to change quickly, he summoned up as much love and forgiveness as he could muster and beamed it to the creatures. Suddenly he found himself at home with his parents and relatives, who were surrounding him and clinging to him, crying. After this dream his problems concerning fear and paranoia (both of which are problems linked to Pluto and Scorpio) began to be greatly relieved.

* * *

Knowledge about the influence of the planets and archetypes can help us to interpret dreams from an astrological perspective and also to discover which areas of life need to be worked on. The dreams themselves may provide many clues.

For instance, dreaming about iron should alert us to look at Mars the sign of Aries in the chart, both of which are linked to weapons and metalwork. This, in turn, may connect with a message about our energy and drive, and ways in which it is utilized or blocked in everyday life. Once the links have been made between the dream symbols and the astrological chart and the correspondences are understood, it is possible to deduce exactly which areas of the psyche and which archetypal energies need closer attention.

To give another example, in a fairly complicated dream from our files, the dreamer was attending a course, and all the subsequent changes in the dream scenery were connected with different phases of this course. In this person's birth chart, courses such as higher education (not schoolwork), came under the ninth house. Here, Pisces was situated on the cusp and therefore this house was ruled by the planet Neptune. This immediately directed us to look at the role the archetype Neptune plays in learning, and in this course in particular, which (in real life) involved apprehending things at a subtle level and translating them back into everyday life.

In the dreamer's chart, Mercury was situated in opposition to Neptune, which showed that the subject's concrete or rational mind might be too critical and sceptical to allow easy access to guidance received from the subtle dimensions. The planetary aspect indicated a possibility of confusion unless information was clearly written down and immediately clarified.

CHAPTER 12

Interpreting Dreams

 ust as we have a great deal to learn if we are to master the intricacies of astrology, achieving a competent level of skill in interpreting dreams takes considerable time and effort. A general astrological forecast which one might read in the daily paper cannot possibly apply to the individual; neither can a general dream interpretation. Each dream is different and unique to the dreamer and, as we have seen, each dream symbol has a meaning peculiar to the dreamer. However, once we have established the groundwork, a whole new world can open up, a world where infinite wisdom can be found.

The Structure of Dreams

The flow-chart system of dream interpretation (described in detail in *Dream Interpretation – The Secret*) to some extent simplifies the process, but there is no short cut to developing the required skills. First, one should study the topic of dream analysis thoroughly, including the works of Freud, Jung and Perls; many interesting books have been written on the subject of dreams, each offering food for thought.

Next, it is essential to develop an understanding of how dreams are structured. This is where we differ entirely from Freudian and Jungian schools of thought. Neither Freud, Jung nor Perls could possibly have known about the structure of dreams, simply because nobody had yet researched the subject. Sleep laboratories and the modern equipment which monitors brainwave activity, for example, are very recent inventions.

Dr Keith Hearne has made some fascinating and pertinent discoveries, reported in numerous scientific articles and in his book, *The Dream Machine*, but many dream analysts remain ignorant of his findings.

For example, Dr Hearne discovered that in a dream light levels cannot be dramatically and instantly changed. It seems that the part of the brain which controls visual imagery cannot make such adjustments in an instant. Therefore, light levels within dreams are likely to increase or decrease more slowly than in real life.

The light-switch effect

Although there are a few exceptions to the rule, if one attempts to turn on a light in a dream, it will not function properly. Usually, it will fail completely, fuse, or only glow dimly. This phenomenon, known as 'the light-switch effect', is particularly relevant during a false awakening (see page 50).

An uninformed analyst could easily make an entirely inaccurate interpretation if a client reported that he was unable to turn on a light during his dream. A follower of Jung might well decide that the dreamer was 'not seeing the light'. Even worse, a Freudian analyst might suggest a problem of impotence.

The scene-shift effect

This is another aspect of dream structure which needs to be understood. Dr Hearne discovered that visual imagery within dreams changes from one scene to the next by the law of least effort, and it does so by employing associative pathways. In other words, in one scene there might be a green man, a blue table and a red apple, then in a flash the scene changes. What is crucial for the analyst to understand is that the man, table and chair will have been incorporated in the next scene, albeit in different forms. For example, the green man could become a green dog, the blue table a blue chair and the red apple a tomato.

For generations, there has been speculation that dreams might follow verbal and visual pathways. Certainly, the scene-shift effect confirms that visual pathways are present. Verbal puns also play a big part in decoding a message. We have come across many dreams that play on words. For instance, in one dream interpretation, it transpired that the word 'cheeses' represented 'Jesus'.

Message-bearing Dreams

Not all dreams lend themselves to interpretation. Lucid dreams, for example, are unsuitable because they are under the dreamer's control. However, it is possible consistently to identify message-bearing dreams, those that are likely to yield a cohesive interpretation.

Message-bearing dreams will, in general, have three main characteristics:

1. They are vivid.
2. They are accompanied by powerful emotions that linger long after the dreamer has woken.
3. The dreamer invariably wakes up at the climax of the dream and can therefore recall its content.

We tend not to remember any boring dreams, unless we are woken during them by external or artificial means (such as an alarm clock). Perhaps such dreams, which carry no significant message, are simply sorting through the events of the day. When a vivid, message-bearing dream has been experienced, the subconscious seems to set off some sort of trigger mechanism, signalling the dreamer to wake up. This ensures that they remember the dream and can study it. For this reason, when we receive a dream report that concludes with the words 'Then I woke up', we are alerted to the possibility that it is a message-bearer.

As a rule of thumb, the more vivid a dream, the more striking the message and (usually) the easier it is to analyse. This is particularly evident with dreams that are accompanied by powerful emotions. The stronger the emotion, the easier the interpretation and the more profound the message is likely to be.

Nightmares

In our experience, nightmares are always message-bearers. During normal sleep, the average person breathes at a rate of approximately ten breaths a minute, but during a nightmare, their breathing rate increases quite alarmingly, sometimes reaching over 30 breaths a minute. As this rapid breathing peaks, it invariably coincides with an emotional climax in the dream, at which point the dreamer wakes up. This awakening is usually accompanied by an increased (sometimes dangerously fast) heart-rate and strong emotions. The content of the nightmare will be striking and hard to forget.

Nightmares are often terrifying, but they can be banished or controlled (see *Dream Interpretation – The Secret*), and they convey valuable messages that can be revealed by analysis. Surprisingly, their meaning is generally not frightening. It is usually fairly important; it may be a warning, for instance, perhaps pointing out that the dreamer is acting unfairly towards somebody during waking life, or following the wrong spiritual path.

The fact that the dreamer will, on waking, go over a nightmare several times and is able to recollect it in detail alerts us to the possibility that the subconscious is trying to convey some kind of message to the conscious mind. Many people find themselves replaying their nightmare throughout the rest of the day until either it begins to fade, or they reach some sort of conclusion or make a decision.

This seems to suggest that the nightmare is forcing the conscious mind to consider it repeatedly, but why? Our theory is that a nightmare compels us to confront pain or mental anguish until it has been exorcized, or until we get the message, even without realizing it.

Interpreting a Dream

First, the analyst must know something about the dreamer. Obtain as much information as you can, including such details as the subject's age, marital status, job and temperament. (You may like to use The Melbourne–Hearne Questionnaire on page 122)

The letter of introduction often contains helpful clues. Clients sometimes list various facts about their age, job, marital status, etc. and then, for no apparent reason, add something like: 'Recently, I separated from my boyfriend.' Experience has taught us that these snippets of information usually have a bearing on the interpretation. They suggest that the client's subconscious is well aware of the meaning of the dream, but cannot fully communicate this to their conscious mind.

Second, write down the dream or, preferably, persuade the subject to supply a written description. (If it is your own dream, describe it and analyse it as objectively as you can, as though it were someone else's dream.) Read the account several times in its entirety, then occupy your mind with something else for a few minutes. It is at this point that an overview of the dream begins to filter through. Study the dream again, all the time relating it to the psychological profile of the client. Continue rereading the dream until you get a 'feel' for it.

Then decide whether the dream is suitable for analysis and can actually be interpreted. For example, does the description end with the 'trigger' words 'Then I woke up'? Remember that dreams which occur during hypnagogic imagery, false awakenings, lucidity and sleep paralysis do not lend themselves to interpretation; they are much more likely to be contaminated by conscious thoughts.

Next, break down the dream into the categories of its constituent parts: setting, action, dialogue, symbols, emotion and any other aspects that seem relevant. Repeat this process for each dream scene.

Now select the most salient points and draw up flow charts for each one similar to the example on page 121. Bearing in mind all theories of dream analysis, try to find a common thread or theme that has links with each flow chart. Remember to look for puns and always bear in mind what you know about the client.

If you find a theme that fits every flow chart, the message behind the dream will reveal itself. However, if the theme can be connected to only some of the charts, start again from the beginning. This process is repeated and checked until the correct interpretation leaps off the page.

Never force an interpretation, or attempt to make part of it fit. This is a particular temptation when analysing one's own dreams, especially if one does not acknowledge one's darker side. It is vital to continue to review every flow chart until the same single theme is recognized in each.

Dreams are usually trying to impart their message in the simplest possible form. Therefore, always look for the most obvious meaning first and try to keep things uncomplicated. Remember that nightmares often carry a pleasant message, but an important one (hence the extreme awakening method which has been engineered by the subconscious).

As a basic example of the flow-chart system, say a client's dream featured his car being stolen amid diversionary tactics, and a person whose face became distorted and changed. You would begin by writing down the words 'stolen car', 'diversion' and 'distorted face'. Looking for the obvious, you might associate a stolen car with a crime against the client; a diversion could suggest deceit, and a face becoming distorted could translate to 'two-faced'. Putting all this together, the dream might be warning the client that somebody is being less than honest and fair with him, which might result in some sort of loss.

Many dreams (but not all) translate into a well-structed interpretation, with a beginning, a middle and an end; in cases of precognition, there is a future, too. On analysis, it is revealed that the dream has set the scene by alluding to a past experience in the dreamer's life. As the dream progresses, there may be some sort of conflict to be resolved; this relates to the present. Finally, the message may suggest a way of overcoming, or coming to terms with, the cause of the conflict; this relates to action to be taken in the future.

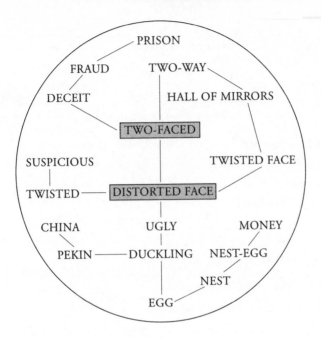

Sort the dream into categories, then draw up a flow chart like this one for each theme or element that is suggested.

What is remarkable about the well-structured analysis is that is takes shape of its own accord; it simply cannot be translated in any other way. However, the actual dream may appear to be a haphazard series of disconnected events, often including bizarre imagery and dialogue.

Parallels can be drawn with the discovery of hieroglyphics. At first, they must have appeared to be random sets of drawings. On closer inspection, it became evident that they contained information which could be deciphered. Once the code was cracked, some fascinating stories were revealed. Dream interpretation is no different: crack the code and a message will come to light.

A well-structured analysis cannot be expected every time. Some dreams seem to be intended simply to offer reassurance or comfort. In these cases, there is often no clear structure, but a general theme that becomes predominant.

THE MELBOURNE / HEARNE QUESTIONNAIRE (MHQ) – FOR DREAM INTERPRETATION

© Copyright David Melbourne and Dr Keith Hearne, 1996.
All rights reserved. <u>Strictly Confidential</u>
Please give as much information as possible, using Block Capitals.

A: The Dreamer

Name . . . .

Address . . . .

. . . .

Usual occupation . . . .

Sex . . . .

Date of birth . . . .

Time and place of birth* . . . .

Education . . . .

Nationality . . . .

Marital status . . . .

Number of children . . . .

Religion . . . .

Interests, hobbies . . . .

Would you say that you are psychic? (i.e. you experience telepathy, clairvoyance, premonitions, etc.)

    Yes / Don't know / No *(Tick)*

How would you objectively describe your personality? (please underline *one* of the 3 categories for items a–g)

    a. Extrovert – In-between – Introvert
    b. Assertive – In-between – Mild
    c. Emotional – In-between – Stable
    d. Trusting – In-between – Suspicious
    e. Serious – In-between – Carefree
    f. Confident – In-between – Worrier
    g. Independent – In-between – Need others

* *This information is useful for solar/planetary/lunar influence research into dreams and dreamers*

First names of people significant to you – e.g. partner, family, colleagues, friends. (These may be represented in disguised form in the dream.) . . . .
. . . .

List matters that are particularly on your mind at this time – in order of concern (most important first) e.g. concerning relationship problems, career, house, illness, money, decisions to make. Give a brief summary:

1. . . . .
2. . . . .
3. . . . .
4. . . . .
5. . . . .

Was/is there something special due to happen a day or two after the dream?

No / Yes (If so, give brief details) . . . .
. . . .
. . . .

B: Dream Report

Provide a *full* account of the dream. Spend some time thinking about your dream and writing the report. Describe *everything* you can remember – even sketch what you saw in some scenes – because sometimes items that seem to be insignificant are in fact very important in the dream analysis. *(continue on separate sheets if necessary)* . . . .
. . . .
. . . .
. . . .
. . . .
. . . .
. . . .

Date of dream:
Night of . . . . Time of dream . . . .
Bed time . . . . Estimated sleep-onset time . . . .

C: Additional Information

Please provide as much information as possible. This categorized data is useful not only in the interpretation, but also for comparison purposes. Various patterns may be noticed between these items in the dreamer over time, or between different people.

Did you take any medication before sleep?
    No / Yes (If so, give details) . . . .

Were the sleeping conditions unusual? (e.g different bed from usual)
    No / Yes (If so, give details) . . . .

What were your thoughts before sleep? . . . .
. . . .

In general, were these thoughts: *(Tick)*
Very pleasant / Pleasant / Neutral / Unpleasant / Very unpleasant?

Would you describe the dream as a nightmare?
    No / Yes

Were the dream events possible in reality?
    No / Yes

Were the events lawful?
    No / Yes

Were the events customary and normal for you?
    No / Yes

Were there links to events that happened in the day before?
    No / Yes (If so, give details) . . . .
. . . .
. . . .
. . . .

Was your sleep more disturbed than usual that night? *(Tick)*
    More disturbed / Usual / Less disturbed

Have you had the dream before?
    No / Yes

Have you any ideas yourself as to what the dream means?

. . . .

. . . .

. . . .

Any other relevant background information: . . . .

. . . .

. . . .

. . . .

Your role in the dream: *(Tick)*
    Observing / Taking part / Both

The setting(s): *(Tick)*
    Indoor / Outdoor / Both
    Familiar to me / Unfamiliar to me / Both
    This country / Abroad / Both / Other

Senses experienced in dream, apart from visual: *(Tick)*
    Hearing / Taste / Smell / Touch / Pain / Sexual

Number of persons/creatures seen in dream: . . . .

Briefly describe these persons/creatures: (Name, sex, age, clothing, behaviour, etc.)

1. . . . .
2. . . . .
3. . . . .
4. . . . .
5. . . . .
6. . . . .

(continue on separate sheet if necessary)

Significant things said by dream characters (indicate who said them): . . . .

. . . .

. . . .

Did you experience sleep paralysis?
    No / Yes

Emotion(s) on waking: ....
....

Psychological state on waking: *(Tick)*
   Very unpleasant / Unpleasant / Neutral / Pleasant / Very pleasant

Amount of activity in dream: *(Tick)*
   Very much / Much / Some / Little / Very little

Amount of noise in dream: *(Tick)*
   Very much / Much / Some / Little / Very little

Colour: *(Tick)*   None / Some / Much / Not noticed

Brightness of dream images: *(Tick)*
   Very bright / Bright / In between / Rather dark / Very dark

Was it a lucid dream? (i.e. where you are actually aware that it is a
dream while you are still dreaming and can control the events)
   No / Yes / Not sure

Did the dream occur on an anniversary of a significant event
for you?
   No / Yes / Don't know (If so, give details) ....
....

Which things stuck in your mind most on waking? ....
....

Rate the stress in your life currently: *(Tick)*
   None / Little / In between / Much / Very much

Weather information (that night): ....

Barometric pressure in morning (if known): ....

Additional questions for females:
How many days after the first day of your latest cycle did the
dream occur? ....

If you are pregnant, after how many weeks into pregnancy did the
dream occur? ....

CHAPTER 13

Astrological Transits

he timing of a dream very often coincides with current astrological transits and progressions, revealing different stages in the dreamer's development. In the majority of cases we have studied, dreams coincide with a major transit, especially when they are particularly striking or memorable. This would seem to support Jung's theory of synchronicity, or meaningful coincidences, whereby external events reflect inner experiences. (For example, at the instant you are thinking about someone, they telephone; it occurs to you how enjoyable a box of chocolates would be, and a friend arrives with one as a surprise gift.)

In the case of dreams and astrology, the effect of synchronicity can be seen in the connections between the dream and the outer-life situation (or the inner thoughts and feelings) to which it refers, the astrological symbolism, and the astrological transit. Even more fascinating is the fact that the dreamer often experiences images which exactly match those of a progressed Moon or a particular transit phase, whether or not they have any knowledge of the complex workings of astrology beyond an understanding of their zodiacal sign.

Progressions are calculated in several ways, but their essential function is to show the slow but steady evolution of our natal energies. For instance, the progressed Sun of people born with the Sun in Aries will, after a number of years, be in Taurus. While they remain Arian in nature, at this stage in their lives they will be seeking to develop a degree of security and stability. The crossover point from one sign to another may be marked by significant dreams which, upon interpretation, can be seen to be indicating the change.

The most commonly used progression method is that of Secondary Progressions. These work on the principle of 'a day for a year', whereby one day of planetary activity is equal to one year of a person's life. This means that the Sun, the Moon and the faster-moving planets will all journey through quite a few sectors of the chart during a lifetime.

Both the Sun and the Moon significantly affect our lives when they progress from one house of the chart to another. In the case of the Sun, the impact of the new sphere of activity will last for around thirty years, and approximately two and a half years in the case of the Moon. The progressions provide the background for the experiences which result from the transits, just as dream settings and atmosphere provide the background for the action of dreams.

There is a fundamental distinction between progressions and transits. Progressions are exactly that: a progressive growth by steady movement through the chart. Transits, which represent the movements of the planets through the sky and affect the natal chart in various ways, introduce new and different energies into the structure of the chart itself. Sometimes the transits are harmonious and complement the energies within the horoscope, but occasionally they challenge our whole psychic system, and it is through their action that we, as individuals, develop new strengths and move beyond our limits.

Dreams related to transits are likely to highlight these changes and challenges to our systems through startling and evocative imagery, whereas those linked to progressions tend to be characterized by a change of mood. For example, our dreams may become more surreal, have more soothing backgrounds, or feature recurrent symbolism.

The timing and movement of transiting planets makes a fascinating study. The slower-moving ones have a triple action, mirroring a complete process of growth. Some transits even have a five-part action, moving backwards and forwards over the same degree five times, which would appear to imply a period of profound growth.

If, for instance, Saturn is moving to occupy the same degree as a person's natal Moon, this happens in three specific stages. The first is when Saturn conjuncts and passes over the degree. It then turns in its cycle to retrograde motion, which is when a planet in its orbit appears to us on earth to be moving backwards. Next, it moves back over the same degree, in the direction from which it came. Finally, it resumes its normal forwards-moving orbit and passes over the degree once more.

The first contact with the natal Moon brings a very specific vibration of energy to the whole system, which will make a deep impression on the individual's subconscious mind. It could almost be described as a shock to the system, because it stimulates a new and very different type of reaction to that of the energy the person had been experiencing. This will certainly be mirrored in their dream life and in corresponding experiences in the outer world.

On the second contact, the person's experience and dreams will once again intensify. This time, the need for resolution will become more pronounced. When Saturn comes into contact for the third time, resulting in yet another peak experience, the individual concerned will have a new understanding of the energy pattern and will probably have discovered or be on the road to discovering how they need to adapt to it.

A transit is not a separate event, but part of a spiral which is renewed with each conjunction, and the stages it goes through in the cycle (first square, opposition, last square and next conjunction) are similar to the phases of the Moon.

Examining the intense dreams that occur at each transit can reveal meaningful information and guidance from our subconscious about what is happening in our lives and the changes we should make. By looking up the transits in an ephemeris (astronomical almanac), or using a specialized computer program, we can discover whether a dream happened on a significant transit night, and record our dreams over the peak period of a transit.

For instance, when linked to the subject's natal chart, the dream about the yellow car and the blocked road (see page 43), was interpreted to mean that she should change her way of thinking. At the time of the dream, Pluto was exactly quincunx natal Mercury and Uranus exactly squared Mercury, highlighting a powerful impetus from the subject's psyche to alter her patterns of thought. In this case, the necessity for change was shown on all counts, rather than by transit alone.

Transits of the Transpersonal Planets

Uranus, Neptune and Pluto are often known as the transpersonal planets, because they are beyond the control of the ego. When they are transiting the Sun and Moon, or the personal planets (Mercury, Venus, Mars, Jupiter and Saturn), there is often quite a major upheaval in a person's life. It could take the form of a change of inner attitudes, ways of thinking, an altered view of incidents which have caused pain and resentment, or a dramatic change in outer experience. As these are the kinds of activity which stimulate major growth, it is natural that the individual should receive some kind of warning from the subconscious mind via dreams.

Uranian transits

The planet Uranus represents the principle of awakening, and of expressing our individuality. It tends to act like a bolt from the blue, with speed and energy, bringing into our lives people or events that have a fast and striking effect and encourage us to change ourselves and our way of life in order to reflect our true individuality. Dreams which are typical of a Uranian transit feature sudden, dramatic or unexpected occurrences or point towards a radical departure from the norm and, hence, to a truer expression of the self.

Neptunian transits

Neptune represents the principle of merging and refining energies, and the energies of the subtle dimensions and imaginative and spiritual realms. It also has the ability to confuse issues, creating a kind of fog or mist over a situation, so that it is difficult to see it in its true perspective. Neptune promotes the urge to escape from the harsh realities of everyday life and merge with the loving embrace of God, or the universal energy (whichever name is appropriate). Neptune is prominent in the charts of many saints and mystics, as well as con artists and crooks.

When Neptune is aspecting our personal planets, we could expect dream imagery from another dimension; it may be spiritual in nature. There may be muddle and confusion, as though we are trying to find the right perspective. We may also attune to other levels of creativity and dream of some imaginative work of fiction or poetry. It is also common under this transit to experience particularly vivid and colourful dreams.

Plutonian transits

The last transpersonal planet is Pluto, which represents the principle of change from one state to another. The changes are usually total, allowing no return to the former way of being. Pluto has the effect of bringing out into the open old patterns of behaviour that have long since served their purpose, so that they can be released. When Pluto is strongly aspecting one of our personal planets, we quite often find that situations from the past play on our minds; people we used to know turn up out of the blue as though to be forgiven, or forgive us, for past misdeeds. The whole period can be rather intense.

Pluto's influence may be expressed in dreams by images of death. One of our clients had dreams about his own death while transiting Pluto was conjunct his natal Saturn. However, as the year progressed and the transit moved through the three phases, it was obvious that he was not about to die, but being advised to change his mental outlook and extend his boundaries. Moving into new areas of life can be frightening, and seem like a form of death at the time.

The following dream illustrates how dream imagery corresponds with changes in transits and progressions. The subject found the imagery particularly interesting because, although she had never been able to ride a bicycle, she was riding one in her dream with ease.

The Dream

✳ *I found myself outside with my two sons, and we were all riding bicycles. I felt very well-balanced and at home on my bicycle, which is strange, as in reality I have never learned to ride one. I felt able to go anywhere and also very safe and competent.*

In my arms, while on the bicycle, I carried a newborn baby. We were perfectly happy together. The baby was about a week old, very tiny and new. I realized that the birth had been a totally happy and pain-free experience. This baby had come into the world with great ease and joy.

I knew that I could cope with everything at the same time and felt very positive about the situation. ✳

Astrological Interpretation

If we look at the client's chart on the date of the dream (30 July 1996), we find quite an astonishing connection between the position of the Moon and the dream imagery. At the time of the dream, her progressed Moon was passing through Libra and the first house of her chart. Not only is the sign of Libra connected with balance and maintaining balance, but the first house of the chart also indicates the beginning of a new cycle. So it seems that the dream perfectly describes 'riding a new cycle'.

The image of the tiny newborn baby suggests the introduction of a fresh element into her life. The fact that she was holding the baby while riding the bicycle and felt completely safe, confident and balanced, tells us that she would be able to move forward with assurance into her new way of life.

Around the time of the dream, transiting Chiron in the first house was in opposition to the dreamer's natal Moon in the seventh, and transiting Jupiter in the fourth house was in opposition to the natal Sun in the tenth. These oppositions emphasized the dreamer's need for balance, in the first case between a home and career, and, in the second, in the sense of healing, helping and nurturing both herself and others.

* * *

Dreams can also mirror inner processes during the period of change brought about by the return of planets to their natal place or by phases in the return cycle. For example, the planet, say Jupiter, starts out at 20° Aquarius, in the eighth house of a chart. At 20° Taurus, it has completed the first square of its cycle, rather like the first phase of the Moon; at 20° Leo, it is half-way through its cycle and is in opposition to its natal place. At 20° Scorpio, it is in its last square or final phase. Back at 20° Aquarius again, it has completed one whole revolution of the chart. In addition, on its journey Jupiter moves through each of the four elements, all of which are at challenging angles to its natal place.

When Jupiter makes aspects to itself, or returns to its original natal place, we have an opportunity to develop the qualities it represents, that part of ourselves which wants to increase our knowledge, to accelerate our growth in any area of our lives. Noting our dreams, and the kind of imagery our subconscious brings to them, at these times, will tell us more about the direction in which we plan to evolve, the subconscious providing a channel of communication to the entire psyche.

You can incubate dreams, i.e. deliberately program yourself to have a significant dream (as explained in *Dream Interpretation – The Secret*) in order to ask your subconscious how best to use and develop certain features of your chart. Say you notice that when Pluto aspects your natal Mars problems ensue in some areas of your life. Using the ephemeris, you could select a time when Pluto is again aspecting Mars and try to incubate a dream at this point, requesting guidance from your subconscious. This can have fascinating results.

An ephemeris will tell you how long the impact of a transit will last. In the case of some of the slower-moving planets, this can be a matter of many weeks either side of the exact transit date. In this case, it would be sensible to incubate the dream on the exact transit date, or within a few days of it.

At the end of a particularly challenging transit phase, when we have gained new insights, resolved difficulties and moved to a higher level of consciousness in problematic areas of our charts, our dreams will reassure us of the benefits of the changes we have made, and confirm that we have progressed to a new level in the spiral of life.

CHAPTER 14

Working with Inner Energies

n this chapter we shall begin to discuss methods of working on inner conflicts in order to attain resolution and healing. Some of them are based on theories employed in psychosynthesis (particularly that of sub-personalities) and core transformation. The use of visualization is also explored. Resolving problems revealed in our dreams and on the natal chart by means of these techniques can produce a metamorphosis in situations that previously represented stifling predicaments.

To carry out these exercises, we need to employ active imagination. This technique was developed by Carl Jung to access the subconscious and unconscious mind, and enabled his patients, while in the waking state, to produce images which gave clues to the contents of the subconscious.

Today, image work and visualization have become very popular methods for effecting changes in various aspects of life, including thoughts and attitudes as well as external situations. These processes highlight the fact that the only way to make a change in our external circumstances is to alter our perspective on life. Our outer reality is the crystallization of our inner world of fluid ideas.

These particular techniques have radically improved people's lives; they require us to concentrate on what we do want to happen in our lives, rather than focusing on what we fear will happen. It is a well-known fact what we most dread quite often happens: we attract it into our lives. If, instead, we visualize and affirm the positive things we desire, even though it may seem unlikely that our wishes will be granted, one day these will materialize.

Imagery can be used to understand and improve virtually every aspect of life. It is a way of working in partnership with the subconscious, and has helped business executives, handicapped people, those with terminal diseases and many others to enhance their lives. This skill is not exclusive to those with a vivid imagination or good visualizing ability.

For example, if you have a pain in a particular part of your body, you can tune into it and ask your subconscious mind to provide an image connected with its fundamental cause. The image you receive may not be directly related to the illness or injury, but will reflect a negative mental attitude, or an inappropriate response to a situation in your life, which is manifesting as physical pain. Once you have understood the image and worked with it, the symptoms generally fade away, bringing relief.

In this chapter, we shall explore ways of using imagery to learn more about our dreams and our natal charts, and thus understand and transform the areas of life which our dreams and charts highlight as being important.

The birth chart, as a map of energy, reveals the interplay of our energies at any given moment. The message of a dream can pinpoint the zone on which we should focus our attention.

For example, one of our clients dreamed that she was standing in a clearing in the jungle, at the edge of a pool of water. On the opposite side of the pool, she saw a group of tribal people. One of them, a beautiful woman with long black hair, walked forward and got into a blue car which was parked just out of sight in the trees. She drove the car quite competently into the pool of water so that it was completely submerged and then, leaving it there, climbed out of the pool.

When we asked our client if she had any ideas about the meaning of the dream, she said she thought it might relate to the fact that she had recently taken up driving.

Looking first at the connection between this dream and our client's chart, we could see that the main theme of the dream seemed to be that of submerging something which was once on the surface. This is particularly relevant to the twelfth house of the chart, as this is where elements of our being become submerged in the subconscious mind. Any planets in this house act on a subconscious level, and their expression is not open to the dictates of the conscious mind. This is the reason why the twelfth house is often called 'the house of self-undoing': we are unconscious of our motives in this area.

In this particular subject's chart, Gemini was on the cusp of the twelfth house, meaning that it was ruled by the planet Mercury, which relates to communication, travel, learning, aquiring new skills, exchanging information, and to short journeys, etc. From this alone, it was possible to deduce that the skill of driving had been transferred to her subconscious mind, indicating that it was becoming an automatic function, rather than one requiring conscious thought.

Sub-personalities

To take the process of interpretation a stage further, an analyst studies the dream and chart imagery to find out whether there are any deeper messages. One particular method, which is suitable for people who do not have a comprehensive understanding of astrology, is to treat various aspects of the dream as different parts of the self. These parts are often known as sub-personalities.

Each sub-personality represents a different element or energy of our being, which needs to be incorporated into one holistic working unit, along with all the other sub-personalities. To use an analogy, it is rather like all the different parts which go to make up the human body. The eye and the stomach have completely different functions, yet work as part of a team, each contributing to the whole. If one part begins to decline and stops working efficiently, the whole body suffers.

We can gain an understanding of some of our sub-personalities by noticing how we react in a variety of situations. We may behave in one way at home with our partners, in another way when at work, differently again while out with friends. There are also certain circumstances in life which call forth a particular part of ourselves; for instance, our behaviour when dealing with business and financial matters may differ from the way we behave when talking to our nearest and dearest. These attitudes are not as obvious or predictable as one might think.

Try asking your subconscious to conjure up an image of yourself in a particular role, perhaps that of a parent. You might, for instance, see a cartoon character wearing a T-shirt saying 'Supermum' or 'Superdad' in bold letters, or a stern schoolteacher, or perhaps a doormat. Whatever image comes into your mind provides clues to the manner in which you conduct yourself in this area of life.

Returning to the dream about the submerged car, the next step was to discover how the dream images were related to our client's everyday life. When we asked her what the image of the blue car meant to her, she put this question to the car itself, asking what significance it had for her in her life. The response suggested that it represented non-verbal communication, such as body language and the kind of general aura we communicate to others, consciously or unconsciously.

Our client then asked the image of the dark-haired woman what she represented. She was told that she symbolized the intuition and instincts, the ability to act from a level beyond the ego or logical mind. When asked why she had driven the car into the pool, the dream image explained she had been trying to drive home the idea of trusting the instincts and intuition, listening to the messages of the inner self, the promptings of intuition. She said she had left the car in the pool to symbolize that there should be more communication between the conscious and subconscious mind, a marriage of the two. Logical thought needed to be wedded to intuitive and creative thinking.

Our client then went on and talked to the pool of water, to see what it signified. It appeared to represent her subconscious mind, which contained a great deal of information that could be valuable to her conscious mind, if it would only ask for it. This approach brought our understanding of the dream to another different level.

We next examined the astrological images to see if we could discover any other layers of meaning. In the dreamer's chart, shown on page 170, Mercury, the planet of communication, was in Taurus, situated in opposition to Neptune in Scorpio and Jupiter in Libra, both of which are rulers of Pisces and, by association, of the twelfth house. This meant that, owing to natal influences, the principle of communication was linked to the workings of the subconscious mind on two counts. Therefore, communication was an important element of the chart and needed to be investigated.

In the earthy element of Taurus, Mercury's receptivity to images or intuitions from other levels of being might be impaired. In order to test this, we requested the client to ask her subconscious mind for an image of Mercury based in the sign of Taurus, showing how it worked in her life and at what level of energy it was operating. As she had a good working knowledge of astrology, our client knew what each of the components meant.

The image she got was of a black cube which seemed to be 'just sitting in a lump', not doing anything in particular. We suggested that she talk to the cube and invite it to tell her about itself. When she did so, she received no response at all; the cube appeared to want just to sit there and not say anything. We seemed to have reached an impasse, so we asked the client to summon up from her subconscious an image of the cube as it would be if it had overcome whatever the obstacle was and wanted to communicate.

She then got an image of a lively, happy cartoon dog, which was very keen to communicate. He told her he had been shut in the box because everyone complained that whatever he said was either stupid, boring or inappropriate; he had literally been 'shut up'.

'Where will you go from here?' was her next question, to which the dog replied that he was sick of having to heed or be mindful of others, as it was repressing his own natural buoyancy. From now on, he declared, he would speak as he wished, and if others didn't like it, they were welcome to walk away.

Next we suggested that our client should conjure up an image for Jupiter in Libra. This turned out to be a rather geometric design of four white squares inside another square on a blue heart-shape, which, in turn, was inside a white circle. The whole arrangement appeared to have been carefully laid out.

She asked the design what energy it represented in her chart and in her life. It revealed that it was interested in everyone being happy and fulfilled; it symbolized a kind of social force which was eager for people to express themselves and enjoy being themselves, comfortable in the knowledge that they were in the right place in life.

Our client's next request to her subconscious was for an image representing Neptune in Scorpio. This produced a kind of vague mist or fog, but nothing definite, which is typical of Neptune. She asked that the image be made clearer while remaining true to its basic energy. This time she got a much clearer picture of a bank of misty water vapour (not fog), with striations of coloured light moving through it. She enquired what part this new image played in her life.

She learned that it was a force beyond the mind which would change the mind when it came into contact with it. It would adjust the mind to the subtleties of other dimensions, but old ways of thinking would have to be left behind. The mind would need to be prepared to merge with this energy, allowing information to come from other levels rather than by the process of logic.

Our client was told that this energy could be used to understand and intuit information and also to draw inspiration from other levels. If ignored, it would bring confusion and muddled thinking. It was emphasized that the energy had a positive part to play, but through neglect had become a disordered force.

So far, our client had discovered three sub-personalities or modes of energy, represented by three planetary energies in her chart. However, this was not the whole story. In her natal chart

Mercury was in opposition to Jupiter and Neptune, which meant that the cartoon dog was working against the geometric design and the cloud of coloured water vapour. We also had to check that the design and the cloud could relate to each other, as they were technically in conjunction but in different signs, and therefore in different elements.

First we asked her to check out the conjunction, to bring the cloud and the design together to see how they communicated. She found that they were on completely different levels and could not make contact. We persuaded her to picture them overcoming this obstacle and communicating very well. Surprisingly, the lively cartoon dog, representing Mercury, the very essence of communication in the chart, offered to act as go-between. He explained that his role was to stay absolutely still and listen to the messages of Neptune from the subtle realms, then pass them on to Jupiter, who would use the information to help others discover their highest potential and live true to their nature.

What started out as a complete lack of communication between the different elements ultimately reached a state where each part was used for the good of the others and of the whole psyche. The process provided our subject with a means of listening to her inner self, for her own benefit and that of other people in her life.

We had also received the important information that Mercury, the planetary principle of communication, acts as a receiver and transmitter of information, listening to subtle clues and intuitions and relaying them to the conscious mind to be acted upon. This strongly supported what we had found out by talking to the dream images.

This process can be carried out with any dream. What was revealing in this case was that, by looking at the chart alone, it was not apparent how rarely Neptune and Jupiter were able to exchange energies, even though they were both rulers of the same sign and should, in theory, have had some connection. It was also interesting to find that Mercury, as a principle of energy, had

closed up and was refusing to communicate. (Mercury was sta-
tionary, preceding a retrograde period of motion, at the time of
birth, so this may have been a contributory factor.)

Once we realize which areas of our lives require attention, we
can continue a dialogue with our dream images on a daily basis
until the issue is resolved.

The next set of exercises comprise ways of evolving the different images, so that they become involved in a growth process. At
times, the energies within us may stop changing and become
frozen, fixed at an age where stress or a trauma caused the particular energy to remain static, or even partially to close down.

The ages of some of our planetary energies, or aspects between
planets, may be different from that of other parts of the chart
which we have consciously used throughout our lives. This means
that if the Sun is trine Jupiter and in opposition to Saturn, the
Sun/Jupiter energy may have continued to evolve with us, whereas
the Sun/Saturn energy may have become stuck at an earlier stage
in our development. This explains why we behave as mature
adults in some areas of our lives and like children in others.

On a conscious level, we may think that we are failing in a
specific area of life and desperately need to improve a particular
skill. However, our higher self may have other ideas. Dreams are
a means of gaining insight into the nature of the path we should
follow. It is essential to keep a regular dream diary, which will be
even more helpful if it includes notes about any special astrological transits or progressions taking place at the time of the dreams.

In the next exercise, we requested our client to visualize the
symbol of Mercury as the lively cartoon dog and enquire how old
it was. The dog replied that he was six. When asked if he was at
this age that he became the black box, the dog answered 'Yes'.

Interestingly, both Uranus and Pluto were transiting the subject's third house when she was six years old. This section of the
chart represents communication, the exchange of information,
early schooling and learning. This would have been a time when
many aspects of her life were changing; there would have been a

lot of pressures which might, at this early age, have caused her to retreat rather than come out of herself. It was likely that Uranus would have disrupted early schooling, and this was confirmed by the fact that our client had moved to another part of the country during the year in question. Her Mercury energy had become stuck at this particular time of life.

Our client then asked the dog if he wanted to come through time to where she was now and move through all the various changes. The dog agreed quite happily.

We asked her to imagine that she and the cartoon dog were walking in the foothills of a mountain. The air was clean and clear and they were going to climb to a certain height (symbolizing her present age). When they reached this level, the dog would have gone through a metamorphosis; he might start changing during the ascent.

They began walking up the gentle lower slopes, through pine and spruce. The incline gradually became steeper and the forest gave way to rockier ground, covered in alpine shrubs and flowers. Higher and higher they went. The dog had already changed: he was now a handsome red setter. At last they reached a large sunny plateau and sat down to rest. The climb was over. Our client inspected her companion with interest and curiosity. The red setter looked at her with a joyful yet serene gaze.

He told her that he felt he understood people better and was no longer frightened of them. He realized that we all share the same basic emotions of joy, fear, confidence and lack of confidence, and he was no longer worried about being inadequate or appearing stupid or inconsequential.

At this point we asked our client to imagine that a doorway leading back to reality had appeared in front of her. She walked through the door with her friend and back into everyday life.

She now had a constant companion with whom she could converse who was a specialist in communication of all kinds. She was free to turn to him whenever she needed advice about how to approach people, make a phone call, write a letter, or about any aspect of teaching, writing or studying. The dog was especially good at listening to the messages of the inner self and translating them back to her, which meant that the dream could now come to a fruitful conclusion.

We persuaded her to try the same process with Neptune, a far more difficult energy to come to terms with. She imagined the cloud of water vapour, with coloured lights flickering through it. When she asked what age it was, she received the information that it was two years old. When she was this age, Neptune was moving through the section of her chart connected with creativity and, perhaps more importantly, she was gradually gaining a sense of self. In the same year, Neptune also made an exact square aspect to her natal Mars, which may have had an early effect on her ability to be assertive.

She enquired how it coped with any problems or pitfalls which arose, and the cloud responded that such difficulties made her feel sleepy; she could hardly keep her eyes open. Our client pointed out that this still happened when important matters required her to concentrate, meditate or sort out her thoughts and feelings. At such times, she would find herself becoming inexplicably sleepy, or increasingly muddled and forgetful, and unable to continue.

She asked the cloud if it would like to evolve from this age and join the rest of the energies. The response was that it would like to stop sleeping so much. Again we used the image of a mountain and they climbed up together from the lower slopes to the large plateau which represented our client's current age.

As she walked up the mountain, the image began to alter, and a figure emerged from the cloud, which now seemed to be made up of coloured strands of vivid, iridescent light. The figure appeared to be a blend of male and female, with clear, sharp energy, in complete contrast to the former sense of confusion. In the presence of this image our client felt she was seeing straight into the essence of things; everything seemed joined together by strands of living colour and light.

When they reached the plateau, the figure assured her that he would be available at all times, but that it would be wise to keep the lines of communication open and use them regularly. This would ensure that the new level of energy would be integrated more easily, without the need to go back to an earlier stage, or the possibility of devolving.

Our client then completed the same exercise with Jupiter, which was represented by the geometric design. This energy was apparently already her current age, so no growing-up was required in this instance.

Finally, we suggested that she imagine all the symbolic images were present and joined hands in a circle with them, in order for them to harmonize and unite. Afterwards she reported feeling extraordinarily clear-minded and calm, with no fuzzy thinking.

The above exercises are simple ways of getting in touch with energies in our lives which would normally be inaccessible. The only real problem may be believing what the energies are saying. Many people feel that they are making it all up. However, the proof is in the results.

It is a good idea to divide your dream diary into two halves, one half for dreams and dream data (add the time and date of each dream for astrological corroboration), and the other half to record the results of any completed exercise, including the images that appeared and what they communicated. Describe how any difficult astrological aspects or impasses were resolved, and note how you develop in each area.

In this way, you will be able to check your progress and also confirm for yourself that there are other levels of reality, which, although they work in different ways to the material plane, can contribute a great deal to our lives. If we are willing to suspend disbelief, these techniques can heal and enhance our lives.

CHAPTER 15

Joan's Dream

his last detailed dream interpretation demonstrates the full potential of using the two methods of analysis in tandem.

The Dream

SUBJECT:
* Joan N.
* British
* Born midnight, 29 November 1918
* Widow with two children
* Writer
* Introvert

✳ *I walked into a large room with a long, oblong dining table. Seated at the table were people whom I didn't know. There was a space at the table, but no chair. I could see two chairs either side of the room. I picked up the nearest one and sat down.*

I noticed two men, both in their mid-thirties. One was on the left, a few places away, and the other on the right, also a few places away. The one on the right was good-looking, with dark hair and aristocratic chiselled features.

Everyone was eating, but I had nothing in front of me. Nobody was serving. I felt uncomfortable, as if I shouldn't be there. Then I heard the man on my left say, very loudly, 'Joan doesn't like milk.'

I was embarrassed and murmured, 'No, I don't, but I'm quite all right.' I felt more and more out of things. I felt a fool, really.

Then the man on the right stood up. He was very tall and authoritative-looking. He made a reference to my not liking certain foods. He said it sternly.

I was flustered but said, 'I do a lot better when it's a hot meal like dinner. I eat a lot of potatoes and veg.'

Afterwards, people began to get up and mill around a bit. Then an unknown girl got up and approached me. She was wearing glasses and was clothed in a bluey-green two-piece. She said, 'I'm a friend of Mary's.' (The Mary I know in real life has led a full, varied life. She is erratic, always one for the men, and doesn't keep in touch much).

I said to the girl, 'I haven't seen her for a long time; October, I think. She flew in and out like she always does.' In the dream, I realized that I'd said October, but I had no idea when I'd last seen her. Then I thought that that sounded like a criticism of Mary and felt I should have asked after her.

At first, the girl hesitated, then said, 'She's seeing the most famous skin specialist in the world.'

Then I awoke and felt worthless for the rest of the day. *

Flow-chart Interpretation

Joan begins by describing a large room with a long dining table, and says there is a space, but no chair. Straight away, this strongly indicates a situation she feels is too much for her (and throughout the dream she refers to feeling embarrassment, etc.).

Nevertheless, she makes a stand and gets her own chair (i.e. creates or claims her own place). Everyone is eating (involved in a social, communal act), but there is nothing in front of Joan and she felt uncomfortable, as if she shouldn't be there (low self-esteem, perhaps?)

The next part of the dream is fascinating and most unusual. There are two men, sitting on either side of a table, left and right. Immediately, this suggests that there are two distinct facets to Joan's male side; a calculating one (on the left), and one which favours authority and aristocracy (on the right).

Had we not known what Joan does for a living, this might have thrown us a bit. (A little knowledge about the subject is crucial.) It becomes clear that the calculating male represents the side of her brain which deals with critical analysis (her work). The other male, though depicted in the dream as being on the right, represents the male side of Joan that deals with everyday life; he is therefore more closely allied to her female side.

When the man on the left shouts, 'Joan doesn't like milk,' she is embarrassed. This indicates that there is conflict between her subconscious and her calculating side. She tries to neutralize the situation by saying that she's all right; she doesn't want any attention drawn to her, or any fuss. She doesn't want conflict.

Let us continue a bit further. The man on the right makes a remark about Joan not liking certain food (certain types of mental sustenance or stimuli, perhaps). Again, there is an element of conflict; in fact, conflict with both males. She becomes flustered, but stands her ground and attempts to ease the situation, saying: 'I do a lot better when it's a hot meal like dinner. I eat a lot of potatoes and veg.'

We have to find out what on earth potatoes and veg could symbolize in the context of the dream as a whole. Because Joan doesn't like milk in real life, her dream uses it to symbolize mental stimuli she would find indigestible. Potatoes and veg denote healthy, wholesome food, of course, so perhaps they represent good mental sustenance.

Now we come to the part of the dream which reveals all the answers. The unknown girl (Joan's female side) is saying that Joan is paying too much attention to convention, or correct behaviour (represented by the male figures). This is creating inner turmoil, the feeling that she doesn't belong, although she has been muddling through, as the dream clearly shows (in each dream situation, she does just enough to either claim her place, or justify herself in her own mind).

Nevertheless, through the girl, Joan's subconscious tells her that she could feel much better, more relaxed and revitalized, by releasing the side of her which she is unconsciously stifling: her female, daring side. That is where her self-confidence lies. Of this, there is no doubt whatsoever. Consider the character traits ascribed to Mary in the dream. It would appear that she is an impulsive, flirtatious, happy-go-lucky person. We are not saying that Joan should emulate Mary, but there is a bit of Mary in all of us.

Let us get back to the dream and explain. Joan says: 'I haven't seen her for a long time; October, I think. She flew in and out like she always does.' This is denial – her feelings confirm the interpretation. She is worried that what she said sounded like a criticism of Mary and that she should have asked after her. Joan has been hiding Mary away and it is a long time (symbolized by 'October') since she let her out. Mary, or that happy-go-lucky female within her, has been stifled, denied and locked away.

Why would a woman who is 'always one for the men' see the most famous skin specialist in the world? To make herself more attractive to men with plastic surgery, toning up the skin, make-overs, etc. (revitalization, in other words).

Let us summarize the meaning of the dream. Joan is suffering from low self-esteem, but manages to do just enough to muddle through (on a mental level). She is paying far too much attention to conventionalism and 'the correct way'. If she listens to what her subconscious is telling her, loud and clear, she will feel more relaxed, far more confident, less nervous and, probably most important of all, revitalized. Joan has been fighting certain facets of her true self, facets that need to be given a place in her life. There is no need for her to be completely 'erratic', like Mary, but she should give freer rein to the happy-go-lucky 'potatoes and veg' side of her nature.

* * *

When Joan saw this analysis, she commented:

> I can relate to the entire interpretation. It was true that I lacked self-confidence, and that the 'Mary' part symbolized my inner self that I would like to be free, but which I kept firmly repressed. In short, very accurate indeed.

As you can see, the flow-chart interpretation revealed a great deal, but, when analysed astrologically, the dream was found to have even more layers.

Astrological Interpretation

Joan has a Virgo ascendant, which means that she is the kind of person who pays great attention to protocol and to doing things in the right way. As the ascendant represents the way people assess us when they first meet us, as well as a particular kind of energy which underlies the many daily activities we undertake, this shows that Joan likes to give the impression of doing things properly. Virgos have an eye for detail and will pay great attention to the minutiae of a project, which is why they are often highly skilled craftspeople: artists, musicians, writers, researchers and so forth.

Joan's Moon is in Libra, in the section of the chart related to personal possessions, values, self-worth and the qualities one has to use in this life. This accentuates the fact that Joan likes everything to look good and to be well displayed or presented. She would rather put a brave face on things than say what she feels and risk hurting someone else's feelings.

Joan's Sun is situated in Sagittarius, in the section of her chart related to writing, communication and the exchange of information, and is conjunct her natal Venus. Sagittarians are not usually known for their tact or sympathy, tending to go ahead and say what they have to say, regardless of whether or not they hurt other people's feelings. In a woman's chart, the Sun often represents a particular type of behaviour that is aspired to. Women quite often relate more to their Moon signs than their Sun signs, although there is no hard-and-fast rule about this.

The Sun in Sagittarius frequently indicates an adventurous spirit and, as Joan is a writer, we suggest that many aspects of her Sagittarian Sun/Venus are expressed through her writing, rather than in real life.

To arrive at a more detailed analysis, we shall now study both the dream and the chart in depth.

The setting for the dream seems to be a social occasion, a meal with people whom Joan doesn't know. This places Joan in the

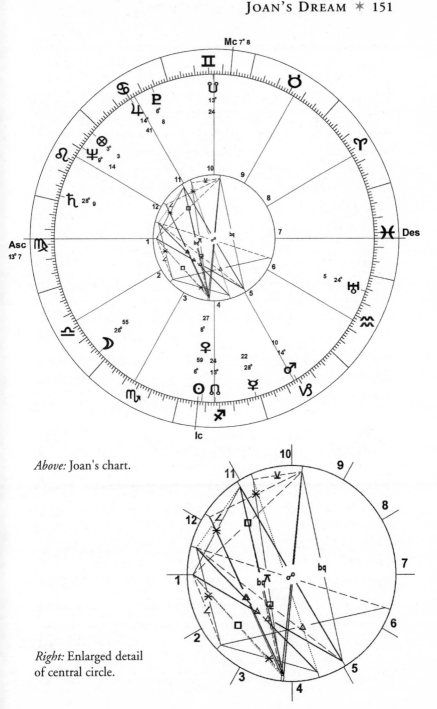

Above: Joan's chart.

Right: Enlarged detail
of central circle.

position of her Moon in Libra, situated in the section of the chart associated with personal possessions, values and feelings of self-worth. Libra, as a sign, is often concerned with how we relate to and interact with others. Joan is linked with her Moon in Libra which, as mentioned above, means that she tries to avoid hurting people, rather than saying what she really feels.

She says that as she approached the table, there was a space but no chair; however, she saw one at either side of the room and, taking the nearest, sat down. Joan, as the Moon, would tend to have a reactive personality. In this instance, she knew that she was supposed to sit down, then saw that there was a space, but no chair. A space had been provided, but nobody had thought it worth putting a chair there for her.

The other people did not have Joan's good manners and thoughtfulness. They didn't even give her a chair: she had to find one for herself. This made her feel worthless, which highlights Joan's feelings about herself. She reacts to other people and, as the Moon's position in Libra reveals, is always trying to make others feel good. She behaves impeccably, yet lacks the confidence to express her true emotions and puts other people's feelings before her own.

By taking a chair and sitting down, Joan tentatively asserts her right to be there, to have a place at the table. However, one also gets the impression that she did this because she felt she was supposed to, not because she wanted to be there.

In the next section of the dream, we are introduced to two of the characters, both men, who are placed a few seats away on either side of her. Joan notes that both are in their mid-thirties. The one on her right is good-looking, with dark hair and aristocratic chiselled features. Later, we learn that he is authoritative and speaks sternly. This suggests that the man on the right, from the detached perspective of the chart centre, represents Joan's Saturn in Leo. Saturn is situated in the section of the chart related to the unconscious mind, mysticism, and areas where conscious beliefs conflict with subconscious ones.

The other man, on Joan's left, corresponds to her Mercury in Sagittarius, situated in the section of the chart concerned with to issues surrounding home and domestic life, early childhood, and ancestral roots.

Saturn represents the principle of authority, a father figure, someone who sets out the rules and maintains discipline. As Saturn is situated in Leo, this would be displayed in an aristocratic or almost royal fashion. The fact that Saturn is in the section of Joan's chart associated with the subconscious mind indicates that this figure represents a subconscious voice, belief or sub-personality.

Mercury represents the principle of communication and exchange of information, and is situated in the section of the chart concerned with mothering and nurturing. This suggests that the message of the dream involves the way Joan nurtures herself, how she feeds herself and makes herself feel good.

Joan goes on to say that everyone was eating, but she had nothing in front of her, and no one was serving. She felt as though she shouldn't be there. In this instance, we again get the idea that Joan tends to react rather than act; she is not one to go and get things for herself. Then the man on the left (Mercury) says loudly that Joan doesn't like milk.

The fact that Mercury is situated in the section of the chart related to mothering, home and domestic affairs, makes this remark even more relevant. Milk is what the young are fed and nurtured on in their early months, giving them the strength to move to the next stage in their development. It appears as though Joan has turned away at a young age from true nurturing. Either she didn't get the nurturing she needed, or she didn't feel as though she deserved it, or a mixture of both. Perhaps her parents thought they were giving her all the love and encouragement she needed, but she may have needed another kind of love and encouragement and so felt bereft. Whatever the reason, it seems that the message concerns Joan's dislike for a certain kind of food or quality of nurturing.

Joan says she tried to cover up her embarrassment at this remark by saying that she was all right, it didn't matter, but she felt like a fool. With a Moon in Libra, ideas about social etiquette, behaving correctly and not appearing out of place are very important. Being in a situation like this one would be extremely painful for a person like Joan.

In the next scene, the man on the right, representing Saturn, stood up and sternly made reference to Joan not liking certain food. As Saturn is situated in the section of the chart related to the subconscious mind, he would appear to be a subconscious figure, a hidden side of Joan, with a secret message. He may be talking about another kind of food, about experiences that Joan has to swallow. Her Moon being in Libra suggests that she will tend to reject this figure.

Perhaps Joan needs to be able to deal more authoritatively with certain situations and show her stern side, although it may not be easy for her to do this. This is the kind of food that Joan does not like: anything which involves harshness or criticism. She possibly dislikes receiving criticism, instinctively trying to do the right thing in order to avoid it. She also dislikes giving it out.

She replies that she does a lot better with a hot meal like dinner, that she eats a lot of potatoes and veg. The hot meal (dinner) is usually the social and formal meal of the day. When the rules of etiquette apply, Joan does a lot better. This again refers to her Moon in Libra.

The scene changes and people begin to move about. An unknown girl, wearing glasses and 'a bluey-green two-piece', introduces herself as a friend of Mary's. Joan adds that, in reality, Mary has led a full life, is one for the men, and doesn't keep in touch much.

Mary represents Joan's Sun/Venus conjunction. This pattern would indicate a person who is decidedly outgoing, somewhat outrageous, with a bold, almost cavalier quality. The Sun is a very vital part of Joan's chart and, as mentioned earlier, much of this side of her nature comes out in her writing. The dream is referring to Joan developing this side of herself, being more daring and outrageous.

This conjunction makes a challenging aspect to her Virgo ascendant. The idea of being outrageous, adventuring and daring strongly conflicts with the reliable, hardworking and fastidious image Joan likes to project of herself.

Joan mentions that she hasn't seen Mary for a long time, since October, when she flew in and out. She feels that, by saying so, she has criticized Mary and at the same time been rude by not asking how she was. Her sensitivity to others is so ingrained that she is always putting herself down in order to make others feel better.

It is interesting that the whole concept of friends in Joan's chart is represented by the eleventh house, which is governed by Cancer and ruled by her Moon, bringing us full circle to the Moon in Libra in the second house, and her feelings of self-worth in relation to others.

In the last part of the dream, the girl hesitates, then says that Mary is seeing the most famous skin specialist in the world. Joan then awoke. She adds that she felt worthless for the rest of the day.

Skin is another property of Saturn, as Saturn is the planet of boundaries, determining where one thing ends and another begins. Remember that in Joan's chart Saturn is in the section concerned with the subconscious mind, and in the sign of Leo. Not only is the sign Leo related to fame (hence 'the most famous skin specialist in the world'), but it is ruled by the Sun, which brings us back to Joan's Sun conjunct Venus in Sagittarius.

Saturn is also very much connected with the ego and the formation of certain conscious qualities and characteristics which make us individual and differentiate us from each other. By attending the skin specialist, Mary is putting on a new appearance (and having it done on a professional basis) in order to look her best, to feel good.

The message seems to be that Joan needs deliberately to develop some of the qualities of her Sun and Venus in Sagittarius, which are represented in her dream by Mary. She would be far happier if she consciously tried to be more bold, confident, adventurous, even outrageous, and didn't worry about what others think of her. The dream is urging her to be more carefree, to adopt a more cavalier or bohemian approach to life.

If we look at the planetary configuration around the time that Joan had this dream, it reveals that she is on the verge of a new cycle in life. Her progressed Moon is currently moving through Virgo and through the section of her chart related to the subconscious mind.

Over the next few months, while the Moon is still in this section, Joan will benefit from looking within and examining the beliefs which have held her back. Meditation and visualization, especially to find inner guidance, would also be good for her. When the progressed Moon moves over the ascendant in early 1997, she will begin a new phase in her life.

Pluto, the planet of change and transformation, has recently entered the sign of Sagittarius and began its transit over her Sun in December 1997. However, Pluto has a profound effect, and its influence for change is often felt as much as a year in advance of the exact transit date. Joan will feel a willingness to shed attitudes and behaviour that have restricted her in the past and replace them, instead, with more appropriate and fulfilling ways of being.

Comparisons and Conclusions

In this dream, the two systems of analysis produce virtually identical results. Both show Joan's lack of self-worth and her need to be more carefree and unrestrained, the only real difference being that the flow-chart method has assigned the two male characters to different sides of the functioning brain. In Joan's chart, the two male characters are actually situated as planetary principles equidistant from her Moon in Libra. They are both aspecting the Moon in a harmonious way, which suggests that their message offers Joan a great opportunity, should she choose to act on it.

The two planets involved, Saturn and Mercury, are also harmoniously aspecting each other. This means that they are working together to provide guidance. Joan is able to tune into her subconscious mind for inner guidance. If she can trust the information she receives, it will nurture her soul and boost her confidence and feeling of self-worth.

The overall message is that Joan needs to develop a more daring and cavalier approach to life. She has been caught in a restricting pattern of behaviour that has limited many aspects of her life.

Energy cannot just disappear: when it is repressed in the chart it tends to find other outlets. It may, for example, be projected on to other people, who then act out the roles the individual feels unable to play, for whatever reason.

Sometimes, as here, the energy does not fit in with the way the person feels they should behave. Ideas about what is acceptable and unacceptable behaviour are usually the result of a mixture of parental upbringing, circumstances and life experience. Habitual behaviour will persist unless the individual gains an understanding of the situation.

In this case, Joan felt that both interpretations were extremely accurate and has fully understood what the dream was trying to convey to her. In effect, her subconscious has given her permission to be free and less constrained, to go wild; this is infinitely preferable to reacting to other people's behaviour and being unable to reveal her real nature.

In fact, Joan has written and had published countless romantic stories and novels in which she has freely expressed this side of herself. We hoped that her creativity would reach even greater fulfilment now that it could participate directly in her daily life.

Several months after Joan received her interpretation, we contacted her to inquire if she had given it any further thought, and if so, had it made any difference to her life. Her response was immediate and very positive.

'Absolutely, yes, very much so,' she enthused. 'It gave me a clue how to carry on, and led to reinforcing my basic beliefs in the message of love taught by Jesus.' She recalled how the holistic interpretation suggested that she would benefit from looking within herself for guidance.

She told us that she now tends to see other people as human beings with problems of their own. She had always had consideration for others, but now she feels the need to keep cultivating the nurturing side of herself. She worries less about what other people might think of her and tries to do what she thinks is right, as long as people are not hurt.

We wondered whether she had taken up meditation and visualization, and Joan explained that she does meditate, although not as often as she would like. She sometimes finds it difficult to relax sufficiently to achieve good visualization, but, when she does succeed, the benefits are evident.

This naturally led us to ask whether the interpretation was right in suggesting that, if she could trust the information received from her subconscious, it might nurture her soul and boost her self-worth and confidence. She agreed that it was accurate: she can now stand up for herself much better and realizes she is not the wimp she once thought she was. She knows that she does get things right, and that she is loved and not worthless.

Finally, we asked Joan's opinion of our holistic dream interpretation. She told us:

It has been of enormous benefit to me. I value myself more, worry less, and give out more love. I realize that my basic principle of love is correct. I give out as much as I can. The interpretation has intensified my life, verifying my faith and my trust in my intuition. And it has encouraged me to do things I wouldn't have dared do before.

CHAPTER 16

Insight into Ailments

n this chapter, we look at dreams in which physical ailments or unconstructive attitudes of mind are represented symbolically, and find out how to verify these images by linking them with the dreamer's birth chart.

The word 'illness' covers a vast range of symptoms that can manifest physically, mentally, emotionally or spiritually. It is increasingly being recognized that the root cause of any form of malaise often lies on a more subtle level than the physical plane, and can be the result of repressed emotions, such as deep-seated anger, grief, resentment or an inability to forgive. The reasons behind even apparently accidental events may be traced through the birth chart. Such incidents frequently act as catalysts, bringing necessary change to an area of life that has been stagnating.

When we are ill, whatever the cause, our entire system is out of balance in some way and needs to be stabilized. The task of the subconscious mind is to maintain a state of equilibrium within our systems. We can see its awesome power at work in keeping our bodies functioning. Our hearts beat, our stomachs digest food, extract the nutrients and take them to where they are needed in the body. Therefore it would not be too surprising if the subconscious also possessed a compensatory function.

One of the many purposes of dreams seems to be to provide just this mechanism. They try in coded language to alert us to areas of our lives where our outlook has become lopsided and needs to become more centred, or to inform us about our body and its current condition. Successful methods of obtaining healing through dreams have been sought for centuries.

In ancient Greece, for example, special temples were built where people suffering from illness could try to incubate a dream which would help them to understand their ailments and find a cure. One of the most famous of these temples was that dedicated to Asclepius, the God of medicine, at Epidaurus.

Many people who went there dreamed of Asclepius himself, who gave them special instructions about using a combination of certain herbs or other healing practices which would promote a cure. One second-century Greek writer, Aristedes, who suffered from many afflictions, including earache, toothache and asthma, was advised in a dream by Aesculapius to take cold baths, ride on horseback and walk barefoot. He is said to have immediately ripped off his clothes in front of an astonished crowd and jumped into a freezing pool of water. Apparently, his symptoms immediately disappeared.

In order to obtain a healing dream, the patient had to go through a rigorous routine which involved cleansing rituals, sexual abstinence and avoiding certain foods which were said to inhibit dreams. These preliminary procedures were probably designed to stimulate the subconscious mind to produce the required dream.

Many people today have also experienced dreams in which their own doctor, or an unknown doctor, has given them help and advice. A man who was undergoing a regime prescribed by a doctor dreamed that his doctor gave him a message about his health and future progress. He promptly forgot the dream and went back to sleep. The doctor appeared again, with the same message; again the patient forgot it. The doctor (obviously a very persistent man) appeared for the third time and gave the information once more; on this occasion he remembered the advice and wrote it down.

Dreams like these do not really need much interpreting, as the message has been given and (unless it is of the cryptic type) is usually quite clear. However, some dreams seem to hint at an illness or imbalance, but the message is veiled in symbolism which is difficult to understand. In fact, it is possible that on some level a large proportion of all dreams are healing dreams which, with a little analysis, would yield answers to many of our problems.

Astrology and the astrological chart can provide valuable insights into such dreams. On the physical level, each sign of the zodiac exemplifies different parts of the body; similarly, each of the planets represents particular bodily functions or processes. Elimination, for instance, is represented by Pluto. To give just two examples, its effect is evident in the daily excretion of waste matter from the body or when a boil comes to a head.

Pluto's influence can also be experienced on an emotional level, such as when pressure builds up within a person, bringing a situation to a head so that toxic emotions can be released, through anger, grief or repentance, for example. Quite often a Pluto transit to one of the planets in the chart, or an aspect to its own natal place, will produce just such a crisis.

The birth chart can tell us where we need to pay attention to our health. For instance, Aries is associated with the head, the eyes and the teeth. People with a strong emphasis on Aries in their charts often tax their minds and, through continual use, frequently endure headaches and eye-strain. They tend to suffer from 'brain fag', where the mind becomes tired out and needs a rest, usually a complete break from any kind of mental work. As the fiery planet Mars rules Aries, Arians are liable to be impulsive and often do not look before they leap, which means they are prone to accidents, especially involving the head.

The chart provides a wealth of information, and it should not be too difficult to link any relevant dreams to the associated areas and find clues about the condition to which the subconscious mind is trying to draw our conscious attention.

One of our clients dreamed that she entered the goat house where her goats were kept, to find one of them lying on the floor with parts of its legs missing. She said that, in the dream, she knew that the goat had somehow eaten its own legs. It was lying in the straw, looking forlorn and completely helpless, with bits of

severed limbs beside it. She too felt a sense of despair. She turned
her back to think more clearly about the situation and to gather
her inner resources, and on looking round discovered that the
goat was completely whole again and full of vitality.

Traditionally, in astrology the goat is often associated with
Capricorn, being half-goat, half-fish. This goat was a pet, and any
sort of pet is ruled by the sixth house of the chart, which is also
the house of health, diet, habits and attitudes to service. Saturn
was in this section of the client's chart, indicating that health, and
matters concerning health, required careful attention. She needed
to ensure that she herself had a good diet and maintained her
health to the best of her ability.

However, Saturn is also the ruler of Capricorn, which was situated on the cusp of the seventh house; this house is connected
with partnerships, relationships and dealings with other people.
This suggested that the symbol of the goat was linked with the
situation of the client's partner. He had recurring health problems
connected with rheumatism and arthritis in particular and, dis-
illusioned with conventional drug treatment, he wanted to be
healed in a more holistic fashion and had therefore decided to
consult a naturopath.

His strict diet, combined with the pain of the arthritis, meant
that he frequently went through what is commonly known as a
healing crisis. The crises affected different parts of his body at different times, according to which areas needed cleansing, and he
would often be unable to do anything other than lie still and rest.
At times he felt quite helpless and, seeing him like this, our client
often had similar feelings.

The dream highlighted this state perfectly, especially the image
of the severed limbs, which is also an ancient symbol of change
and transformation. Dismemberment often occured in visions at
times of particular initiation ceremonies. The candidate would
have to endure this distress before being put back together again.

The decisive moment was when the dreamer turned her back
on the goat in order to think about its predicament without

being overwhelmed by the animal's forlorn condition. It seems that the dream was trying to tell her to see the situation from a new perspective. This change of attitude appeared to work: looking back, she discovered that the goat has been made whole again and was full of its natural energy and vitality.

The dream's first message to our client was that a change in attitude was required in order for the situation to resolve itself. It is intriguing to note that it was she, and not her partner, who had to make this change. Quite often, the seventh house of the chart shows some of the expectations we project on to other people. Perhaps the dreamer could not cope with feeling helpless herself, preferring to do anything rather than appear like that. She may have been drawing into her life people or situations that exemplified helplessness, until her own attitude to it had been altered and worked upon.

The dream's second message was one of reassurance: her partner would win through with his healing diet and emerge at the other end feeling whole and vital again. Her dream also assured her that an intuitive understanding of the situation would bring healing to them both. An interesting point is that resolution came when she stopped looking at the problem from outside and turned within for an answer.

One issue remains: the reason why the goat had eaten its own legs. In this case, the legs symbolized support and, more importantly, mobility. This clue suggests a negative and self-perpetuating dilemma. In addition, the goat is often a symbol for the shadow side of our nature (which partly explains the term 'scapegoat'), so the goat in the dream might represent a previously unacknowledged side of the dreamer. Total helplessness was a condition she found quite repulsive at times, to the extent of feeling annoyed with people who seemed helpless and apparently unable to come to grips with their lives.

Therefore, the dream demonstrated her inability to come to terms with part of her shadow which was eating away at her, rendering her helpless in ways not obvious to her at the time. In the horoscope, the shadow is represented by a variety of aspects, but any planets in the seventh house and the ruler of the seventh are indicators of the elements in our lives we either despise, deny, or project on to others. In this case, Capricorn was on the cusp of the seventh house.

For many of us, our greatest need is to reconcile ourselves to our own shadow; if we cannot, this may cause problems which may lead to ill-health. Coming to terms with our shadow side will heal us and make us whole again. Realizing that we have unconsciously contributed to our problems, we will no longer be tempted to blame them on others.

The shadow is another archetype of the self, which tries to maintain a balance between our light and dark sides. The more pure and angelic the image we paint of ourselves, the darker and denser our shadows often are. An example would be the fiery preacher who self-righteously threatens his congregation with eternal damnation for their sins (which are the ordinary foibles and vagaries of all human beings) but is secretly guilty of far more serious offences.

By using the dialogue exercises illustrated in Chapter 14, we can begin to work on our shadow, bringing the darkness into the light. At first we may be shocked by what we find, but we can then move forward in our lives, assimilating the aspects of the shadow we have discovered into our daily existence.

In our client's case, this would mean honestly identifying the areas of her life in which she felt helpless, and acknowledging that she could reduce or eradicate her sense of powerlessness. By overcoming smaller problems, she would gradually be able to create change in the larger issues of her life. In this way, the self-perpetuating dilemma would gradually be resolved, allowing true healing to occur.

CHAPTER 17

Resolving Dilemmas

 reams mostly seem to present us with a paradox, a dilemma or a question. They tend to illuminate the areas of our psyche we need to attend to, bringing them into balance and making their wisdom part of our everyday life. Very little will be achieved if we dismiss our dreams as strange fragments from another dimension. The more we work with them, and with the issues they bring to our notice, the more of our potential we will be able to develop and bring to fruition.

Interpretation is the first step. The next step is to implement the advice revealed by the analysis and, using the dream imagery, to introduce changes that will put us more in harmony with our true nature.

In the next dream, a woman is receiving healing from a friend:

✳ *I was at a concert, in the audience. A friend and his wife were there. There were lots of people around, and a great buzz of talk. It was during the interval, and I was sitting on a chair, leaning forward with my head down by my knees. My friend was giving me healing after I had said my back hurt. The feeling of the healing energy was so powerful that it nearly knocked me off my feet. It seemed to travel down a path of pain to the core of the problem. He said it might feel worse for the next day or so. The healing was to a place at the base of my spine where I was injured as a child during an accident, and it seemed to reach the place of this old injury.* ✳

On one level, this dream gives a clear message that the dreamer may be able to get help for a long-standing condition from which she has suffered in the form of healing.

However, the message of a dream is usually far more complex and additional information may be obtained by linking the dream to the subject's birth chart. This will give precise clues about its deeper meaning and any course of action it may be recommending. By looking at the chart as a whole, we may also discover other ways of resolving the issue highlighted by the dream.

Healing can have many meanings, from curing physical illnesses to balancing unhealthy attitudes of mind. Usually, for healing to be complete, the mind, body and spirit need to be included, as physical illness often manifests as the last and most visible effect in a chain of hidden causes.

Speculation about the root cause of a problem can be largely avoided by examining the client's birth chart, from which detailed information can be gleaned about the invisible workings of their psyche. If, for example, there are a lot of oppositions in their birth chart, they would also have conflicting elements in their nature. They would swing between one idea and another, or one extreme and another, and frequently find themselves in open conflict with others. They may feel as though others are projecting needs or expectations on to them, while they, unknowingly, are simultaneously projecting these demands on to others. The tension which such situations can generate quite often leads to physical illness of one sort or another.

An example would be a difference of opinion with a neighbour, in which both parties believe they are right, each accusing the other of behaviour of which they themselves are guilty. If both are determined to prove themselves right, a great deal of tension could be produced which, if prolonged, could result in one or both of them developing such symptoms as headaches and, more appropriately, 'a pain in the neck'.

Those with many oppositions in their chart who repeatedly find themselves in confrontational circumstances may benefit from transactional analysis, in which the different types of exchanges between people are looked at in depth and the 'pay-offs' for persisting with defeating behaviour are clearly spelt out.

This kind of group work promotes a greater awareness of relationships with others and should, if successful, lead to a healthier and more open set of associations and the ability to understand when problems are being projected on to others and how this can be overcome.

However, the individual's entire chart needs to be studied in order to decide if transactional analysis is the best way forward. Another approach may cover more of the problem areas in their chart, or reach a deeper level of healing.

In one dream from our files, the subject found herself in a besieged city and suddenly decided to save herself by leaving instead of dying gloriously with her comrades. This dream episode can be linked to the second and eighth house axes of her chart. The besieged city implied crisis, which came under the eighth house. Cancer, ruled by the Moon and situated in Aquarius in the second house, was on the cusp of the eighth house, and Pluto was situated in Leo in the eighth, in opposition to Jupiter in Aquarius in the second.

This suggested a dilemma concerning a situation which had perhaps become hopeless. The circumstances may have involved deep emotional bonds, joint ownership and resources or family resources. Alternatively, the dream might have indicated an area of the dreamer's self which had become isolated, marooned or besieged by other elements, and where a deep change or transformation was needed.

In contrast to Pluto in Leo in the eighth house, all the planets in Aquarius in the second pointed to sharing or going through things with others, keeping in mind the group or the circle of friends. Possibly this meant maintaining a group spirit and a sense of comradeship and the lessening of the individual's contribution for the sake of the group.

In the dream, the subject decided to save herself rather than die gloriously with her comrades. Tying this in astrologically seemed to show that her psyche was preparing her for a major transformation in her life. Quite often, when associated with a group, we tend to maintain the level of awareness and identity of the group; our natural inclination may be to progress away from the group, but we may find it diffuclt to do so. Perhaps the dream was conveying the idea that in order to be able to continue and change, the dreamer needed to take some action for herself and her own life, rather than conforming to the rest of the group.

Here, the idea of healing implied finding her own purpose and taking on new ideas that reflected her own personal development, rather than group dynamics. Working on these issues would restore the dreamer to a feeling of well-being and wholeness.

The chart revealed an over-emphasis on groups and group ideals and values, and on others at the expense of the self. For a more balanced viewpoint, the dreamer needed to take more time to evolve her own path, distinct from the wishes or values of others. This would enable her to work successfully in group situations without losing the sense of her own purpose. Healing on this issue would then be complete.

A commonly experienced dream involves being chased by something, or fearing that if we enter a certain place an appalling calamity will befall us. Usually, the presentiment is that we will be attacked and die. In dreams of this kind, the subconscious mind seems to act as a teacher as well as a healer. It creates extremely realistic scenarios in which we are faced with a choice between seeing the conflict or frightening situation through to the end, or escaping from the dream (by waking up, for example) before the dreaded event occurs.

One dreamer found herself climbing up the main cable of a suspension bridge in a bay area. She was running from a hostile crowd on the beach, some of whom were following her into the water and on to the bridge. She knew they meant to kill her and, feeling doomed, she purposely fell into the water, as she knew this would put an end to her predicament. She then awoke safe in her bed.

Another subject kept dreaming of being chased by a large, very menacing tiger. Each time she had this dream, she would wake herself up at the crucial point, just as she could feel the tiger's breath upon her legs.

On one occasion, she again found herself in a jungle being chased by the same tiger. Again, it was catching up on her and she could feel its breath on her legs. This time she realized that she could not keep running from the tiger: she had to turn around and face it. She did turn, and stared it right in the eye. At this, it became positively tame, almost like a pet, and they continued the journey through the jungle together, feeling happy to have made each other's aquaintance at last.

Unfortunately, the dreamer did not keep a dream diary, so there was no record of the dates on which this dream or her previous dreams had taken place. It would have been interesting to discover whether the dream in which the final resolution occurred could be linked to planetary transits or progressions.

Dreams frequently highlight the opposites we need to reconcile in our lives in order to become whole. For example, one woman dreamed that she was walking up a winding staircase inside a large building. As she walked up the stairs, she decided that she would express deep love and reverence to the next person she met. She looked up and saw a man with dark curly hair, dressed all in black, coming down the stairs. As he passed her, she said, 'I really love you.' His sneering reply was, 'And I really hate you.' She awoke feeling quite hurt and shocked that her intention to express love had resulted in such a wounding response.

The energy of opposites in dreams can sometimes be traced to a direct opposition in the natal chart, which was the case in this particular situation. The dreamer's chart (see page 170) revealed an exact Pluto/Venus opposition, with Venus at 29° 45' Aquarius and Pluto at 0° 3' Virgo. Venus was conjunct the MC at the top of the chart, while Pluto was conjunct the IC at the bottom of the chart.

It seemed, therefore, that the dreamer was identifying with the Venusian and Aquarian qualities of love, beauty and harmony and neglecting or refusing to identify with the Pluto energy of

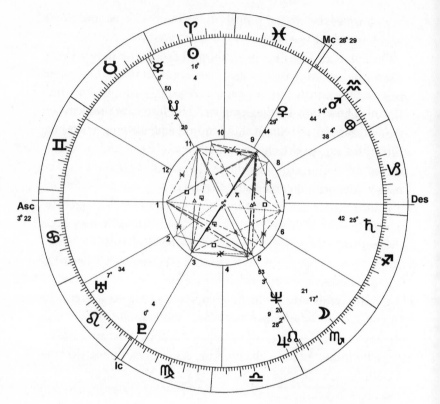

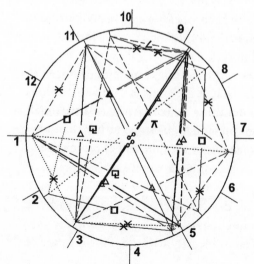

Above: Venus and Pluto are clearly in opposition in this chart; the subject's dream about a staircase revealed unresolved issues surrounding the darker, shadow side of her psyche.

Left: Enlarged detail of central circle.

change, transformation, elimination or clarification of stagnating and repressed energy personified in the male dream figure.

In mythology, Pluto is often linked to the underworld and, in astrology, to the subconscious and unconscious mind. Plutonian issues are frequently power issues, concerning manipulation and control. Those with a strong emphasis on Pluto have problems in letting things go, in relinquishing control and allowing situations to resolve themselves or people to be themselves.

When Pluto is in opposition to Venus in the chart, relationships will tend to involve many shades of darkness and light. In any relationship, the deeper issues cannot be ignored, and will eventually surface in order to be resolved. Until this happens, a relationship may be that of the manipulator and the manipulated. There may be power struggles, one person taking on the aspect of the dark, and the other the light.

The metaphor of the staircase was very appropriate here, as stairs connect one level with another. While the dreamer's ego was identifying with goodness and love and imagined herself to be moving upwards, her darker qualities, which had been repressed, were in fact descending to a lower level.

In order for healing to take place, the dreamer would need to work with the energy of the dark male figure, perhaps by carrying out some of the exercises in Chapter 14, and pay attention to relationship issues, including the roles played both by herself and her partner.

A great deal of commitment is necessary if we are to work with dreams as messages from the higher self and bring them to resolution. Nevertheless, the resulting self-discovery and personal growth, achieved through our inner guidance rather than any external influence, more than justify the time and effort involved.

CHAPTER 18

Life Paths

uite often, our path in life does not proceed in a straight line but tends to meander. Just as a captain keeps the ship on course by a series of changes which continually nudge it in the right direction, we sometimes veer off to the right or to the left, moving in directions which may seem diametrically opposed to our central purpose. We may lose sight of our path altogether, stray along in the wrong route, or have no idea what our purpose in life is – we may not even care.

There is no doubt that when we are 'on the right path', life in all its aspects seems to flow more harmoniously. We feel as though we are in the right place at the right time, doing the right thing. We are also happier and more fulfilled, and frequently regard our work not just as a job but as something we really enjoy.

Our purpose in life may not be an earth-shattering one; it may be simply to capture beauty through painting or photography. If this is what makes us feel fulfilled, we will probably be very successful. Finding our purpose, in essence, means doing what we love to do, whether this is caring for others, forging ahead into new areas of thought, inventing things, or a mixture of tasks.

At times, our search for meaning can be delayed, especially if transforming events need to happen in order for us to gain the right knowledge to continue along our life path. This is where the value of writing a regular dream diary becomes apparent, acting as a constant link with the subconscious mind, and recording our progress.

Significant changes may be heralded in the birth chart by transits to the IC/MC axis, especially if aspected by one of the outer planets, such as Uranus, Neptune or Pluto. We also experience many life changes when one of these planets conjuncts our Sun by transit. Transiting planets can influence us in a variety of other ways, depending on which areas of our lives need change. For instance, if the outer planets aspect Venus by transit, this will have a profound effect on our relationships, which in turn may instigate a major life change.

The following dream (with a much shortened interpretation) seems to highlight just such a change in attitude, possibly affecting the dreamer's life path. The emphasis on the ninth house of the chart suggests a precognitive element to the dream.

The Dream

* *I was with a friend, and we may have been youthful. I was in an unfamiliar house, presumably my friend's. He had an astronomical telescope (I used to have one when I was about ten). We seemed to be in an upstairs room which had windows on all four sides. It was deep twilight and we were looking south toward a big full moon, pale gold against a mid-blue sky.*

He gave me the telescope to look through. I tried to line it up on the moon, but I was having trouble keeping the telescope still, as it wasn't on a stand. I was trying to rest the far end of it against the window-pane to keep it steady.

I was a little disappointed that it didn't seem to increase the apparent size of the moon by much. The moon drifted rapidly across the sky from left to right, so fast we had to move the telescope to another window to follow it. I then noticed there was something big and dark silhouetted in front of the moon. We were trying to figure out what it was, because its outline was irregular and it seemed to cover two-thirds or three-quarters of the moon's disc.

Then it moved off toward the right, leaving the moon's disc, and as it came into the full moonlight, I saw that it was two enormous red roses, linked together and surrounded, just below the flowers, by a spray of green leaves. They flew off silently toward the right, a bit

like enormous spaceships, on a horizontal path, seeming quite close
to the ground, although, of course, they would have been utterly
massive. I watched them in awe and amazement as they sped away,
and that's all I remember. ✳

Astrological Interpretation

The dreamer's chart showed the Sun in Gemini situated in the section connected with broadening horizons, pushing back boundaries, whether in terms of physical travel or travel within the mind, accessing new layers of knowledge and consciousness. The Sun, Mercury and Uranus in this section revealed that the dreamer was always thirsting for new knowledge, ahead of time in his ability to understand and work with new concepts of thought.

The Moon was situated in Sagittarius, in the section of the chart connected with learning, communication, writing and teaching. This meant that it is in this person's nature to tell others about new ideas, enrich their understanding and bring them fresh ideas about the meaning and mysteries of life, and, as Sagittarius is also the symbol of the clown or buffoon, to bring a sense of humour and lightheartedness to the whole subject.

When analysed using the astrological chart, the dream seemed to imply that the next step on this person's path involved accessing more of his intuitive side, following his inner wisdom rather than the dictates of logic alone.

The focus of the dream appeared to be related to the ninth house of the chart, due to the nature of the symbolism and the activity involved. The opening of the dream concerned the dreamer and a friend; they 'may have been youthful'. They were looking at the Moon through a telescope. The function of the telescope is to expand our horizons, to bring things that are distant nearer to us so that we can familiarize ourselves with them. The sign on the ninth house cusp was Gemini, and the Sun was also situated in Gemini. The symbol of Gemini, the Heavenly Twins, probably related to the two youthful friends. One aspect

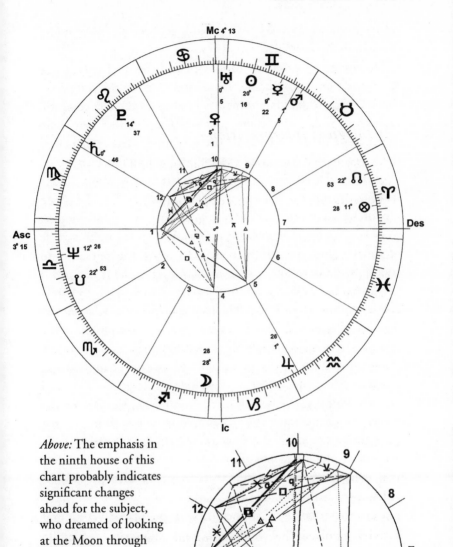

Above: The emphasis in the ninth house of this chart probably indicates significant changes ahead for the subject, who dreamed of looking at the Moon through a telescope.

Right: Enlarged detail of central circle.

of the dream seems to suggest the purpose of the dreamer, and his place in the larger scheme of things.

The imagery of the full Moon formed the next part of the interpretation, and became the central focus of the rest of the dream. The dreamer had difficulty in keeping the telescope still enough to look at the Moon, and was disappointed that it did not increase the Moon's overall size very much. Trying to analyse the Moon in this way did not seem to teach him much about it.

To make matters worse, it began to drift rapidly across the sky from left to right. This movement from left to right has been identified as a change from left-brain activity, or the more logical way of operating, to right-brain activity, or a more intuitive mode of functioning. The dreamer had to move the telescope to another window to follow the Moon's progress, and it was at this point that he noticed the object covering two-thirds to three-quarters of the Moon's disc. The language used was very precise; the words 'figure out' also indicate a very logical approach to the situation, confirming the dreamer's left-brain approach.

The next scene in the dream was so awe-inspiring that all attempts at logic fell away. As he watched, the dreamer noticed that the object moved away to the right from the face of the Moon. As it came into view, it was seen to be two enormous red roses, linked beneath the flowers by a spray of green leaves. Because the bright red and green colours symbolize new life, they were even more incongruous in connection with the Moon, which is generally thought of as a dead place.

Interestingly, roses are connected with the planet Venus, and Venus was situated in Cancer in the dreamer's chart, so the rose against the Moon was an apt image. Also, the position of Venus, conjunct Uranus and the MC, all situated in Cancer, indicated a possible change in path and purpose, or perhaps a realignment with the true path.

The ninth house is concerned with future-orientated affairs and thus with prophecies and forthcoming trends, which could mean that a precognitive element was involved. This dream was possibly foretelling a profound change in life-style, letting the dreamer know that one phase of his life was over (the full Moon representing harvest) and a new one was about to begin.

This new phase seemed to be linked to tapping the intuitive and mystical side of himself, rather than the logical and analytical side, and would bring him to new frontiers of knowledge. The dreamer might, for example, be presented with a life-changing opportunity, or be influenced by someone who displayed strong right-brain qualities. In many ways the dream's message suggested an explosion of life in what had been a somewhat empty environment. However it came about, it was sure to have a great impact.

* * *

An individual horoscope contains many clues about the kind of path or occupation that would best suit the subject. To gain a true picture, the whole chart needs to be studied and the characteristics and inclinations of the person concerned linked and compared. For instance, the fact that the Sun is in the second house of the person's chart doesn't necessarily mean that they should work in a bank, but it could indicate that they are searching for a true set of values, because they want to discover what is most important in life. This would also affect their attitude to money.

Each of us is unique, with a distinctive set of talents, and it is impossible to categorize people. There is a story which conveys this idea perfectly. A man stopped to look in a junk shop to see if there was anything of value there. He noticed a carved and bent piece of wood, some bits of wire and a few wooden pegs. Someone else came along to gaze in the window, saw the same items and rushed in to buy them.

'What are you going to do with all that rubbish?' asked the first man.

'Call at my house and I'll show you,' was the reply.

When he arrived, the first man found the other playing a beautiful harp made from a carved piece of wood, some bits of wire and a few wooden pegs.

How often do we ignore elements of ourselves, saying, 'This part of me serves no purpose'? When all the pieces are put together, we become truly ourselves, able to express our unique abilities.

This underlines the importance of understanding all the energies in our birth charts, getting to know how each part of us works and then bringing the parts together to function harmoniously. The qualities we bring to the way we live are more important than what we actually do or create. Some of these qualities may be better expressed through one activity than another. For instance, someone who has a capacity for precise, analytical thought may find their best expression in scientific research.

In a short dream extract from our files, the dreamer was visiting her grandmother in Glasgow. However, it was not just her grandmother but also her great-grandmother; the figure appeared to represent both. The dreamer felt she was not paying this image much attention, but she did not mind, as the personage seemed about to leave or to die. When it was time to go, the dreamer realized that she had come by car and could not remember where she had left it. The rest of the dream involved her search for the car, which she hoped had not been stolen.

The dreamer was interested in identifying any family and ancestral patterns which might still be influencing her daily life and the present generation of her family, and she had mentioned various aches and pains which had been bothering her. She thought the dream might be saying that it was time to take leave of certain conditioned patterns and bodily tensions which had been handed down to her by her female ancestors. She also felt that it contained a warning about neglecting her vehicle, i.e. her bodily vehicle.

Linking the dream into the dreamer's chart revealed other possible meanings. The grandmother was represented by the seventh house. The cusp of the seventh house was in Gemini, with Mercury, the ruler, situated in Aquarius in the second house, conjunct Venus and the Moon, also both in Aquarius. Uranus was situated in Cancer, forming a trine to the Sun and MC. These two aspects both highlighted the same feature. The fact that Mercury was conjunct both Venus and the Moon in Aquarius showed that the grandmother represented a strong feminine influence from the past.

All this suggested that the dreamer had certain characteristics or mental attitudes which were important but needed to be updated or put into a modern context. Something valuable seemed to be contained within the grandmother figure; its old form was about to die or leave, but its essence had a strong bearing on the dreamer's current attitudes or life-style.

This idea was supported by the position of Uranus in Cancer, which indicated taking the best from the past and putting it into a contemporary framework. Linking the grandmother figure into the chart revealed that it was the old form of some attitude, talent or behaviour was about to disappear, and its essence needed to be reformed or reincarnated. This pattern was also connected with the dreamer's path forward in life and her life purpose, as shown by the trine from Uranus to the midheaven and Sun, both indicators of life path and purpose.

The next part of the dream reinforced the first part. The dreamer realized as she was about to go that she had lost her car, and didn't know where she had left it, or if it had been stolen. Cars or vehicles are related to the third house of the chart, which contained the dreamer's Sun in Aquarius (also on the cusp). Perhaps the dream was hinting that she had lost track of her real purpose, or that it had been stolen from her in some way. When we have left our path, we often develop general signs of disharmony, which can range from things going wrong in our lives, or a feeling of despondency to vague but persistent physical malaise.

Looking for the car could be translated to mean that the dreamer was searching for her purpose. As the third house of her chart was also connected with the mind and mental processes, one aspect of her purpose seemed to be communicating new ideas and new lines of thought, and, more specifically, futuristic, innovative theories which would be of benefit to society.

As we become more conscious of our purpose in life, we may cease to identify with traditional roles and discover completely new elements within ourselves for which no set role exists. Working with our dreams and the energies inherent in our natal charts will give us the courage to move into these new areas and manifest them in our lives.

The purpose behind writing this book and combining both our methods of dream analysis was to establish a new and exciting way of accessing the tremendous potential which is hidden in the subconscious. We would like to ask you to continue this work, to try to build on and develop our discoveries. Recording dreams on a regular basis, as well as gaining an understanding of astrology, psychology, mythology and basic dream interpretation should all bring rich rewards.

The recording of dreams forms the fundamental basis for all research as it is only after significant periods of time that recurrent themes and images will begin to present themselves. When linked with astrological data and the movement of the planets it is possible to uncover some intriguing results which have been explored in this book. However, there are many more aspects of research to be explored, such as:

* Noting over a period of time (say over six months) just how many features of dreams can be linked to the natal chart, and how many represent movements of planets or progressed planets, or even asteroids and other chart points.

* Recording as many of the night's dreams as you can, to find out how many different themes can be isolated and linked to the chart, current transits or progressions. Do certain types of dream relate to specific times of the night?

* Researching astrological or astronomical factors which contribute to lucid dreams, or other aspects of dreaming.

These are only a few ideas for further study and research, and are only limited by imagination. Good luck.

Appendix

If you wish to gain a basic understanding in the subject, information on courses led by both authors can be obtained from the address at the back of the book. The notes in this section may also be of help.

Description of the 12 houses and the areas of life with which they correspond.

The birth chart *(opposite)*

A birth chart is a map showing the planetary positions at the time of birth. The planets, ascendant/descendant, IC/MC, and other points and parts of the chart symbolize the psyche of a person and their emotional, mental, physical and spiritual state. This diagram shows a typical birth chart with the three different planetary placements: in the central circle the positions as they were at the time of birth, progressed planets in the outer circle and transiting planets around the outside of the chart.

Interpreting the birth chart The astrologer starts by looking at the planets in the inner circle, to understand the dynamics of the individual. For instance, by looking at the position of the Sun in terms of sign, house and aspects reveals the persons underlying essence and purpose in life. A study of the Moon position would reveal much about a person's emotional side, and their ability to nurture and sustain themself and others. A study of Jupiter would tell us about our opportunities and those areas of our lives where we have faith in ourselves. Saturn, on the other hand, says a lot about a deepest fears and insecurities.

Transits, progressions and dream life The term TRANSITS relates to the movement of the planets in the sky at any given time after the birth date. As they symbolically move around the chart, they aspect the natal planets. The movements of the transiting planets affecting those in the natal chart reflect movements of energies within our being. Changes within are reflected by changes in our everyday lives and are very much reflected in our DREAM LIFE.

Secondary PROGRESSIONS, the method used in this book, are based on the movements of the planets in the days shortly after birth, whereby each day is the equivalent to one year of life. The progessions of someone who is 30 years old would be calculated from the position of the planets on the 30th day after birth. Progressions reflect a more evolutionary growth, a natural progression. As progressed planets make aspects to natal planets this again brings about changes within the individual and most certainly affects the dream life.

Transits and progressions are used when forecasting future trends in a person's life, or to ascertain the influences that were involved in a particular situation in the past. Once the initial birth chart has been drawn up, it can then be used to look into any area of a person's life.

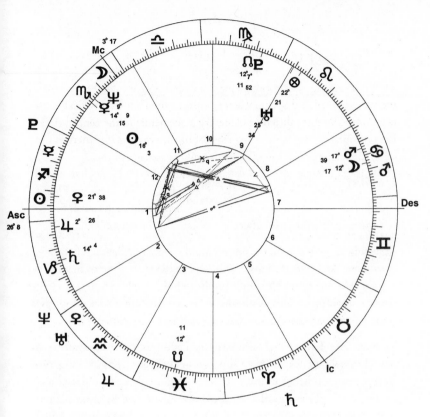

Above: Example of
a typical birth chart.

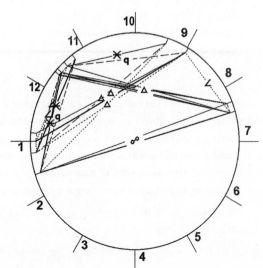

Right: Enlarged detail
of central circle.

Glossary

Angles The angles are four sensitive points on the birth chart which equate with the ascendant, descendant, IC and midheaven. Planets positioned next to these points, either at birth or through transit or progression, have a powerful effect on this area of the person's life.

Ascendant The ascendant represents the sign and degree of the sign that was rising over the eastern horizon at the exact time of birth. The sign on the ascendant also corresponds to how people view us on a first-impressions basis, and to the mask or persona which we adopt as a buffer between others and our deeper nature.

Aspect The distance between two planets or points in the chart measured in degrees. Each aspect shows how different parts of the person relate to each other. For example, Mars conjunct Venus would indicate a specific combination of the principles represented by these planets. There are seven main aspects: conjunction (0°); opposition (180°); square (90°); sextile (60°); trine (120°); quincunx (150°); sesquiquadrate (135°). (See individual entries for the specific meanings of these aspects.)

Axis The birth chart has two main axes, one running horizontal and one running vertical. The horizontal axis is represented by the line joining the ascendant and descendant and the vertical axis by the line joining the IC and midheaven.

Birth chart The birth chart, also known as the natal chart or horoscope, is the astrological map drawn up for a person, calculated according to the exact time they were born.

Conjunction This aspect occurs when two planets occupy the same degree. It can be found on a birth chart when two planets were close at the time of birth, or it can happen by transit or progression.

Cycle This represents a complete revolution by a planet. This may be one complete passage through the chart from the ascendant through 360° and back to the ascendant, or the planet's own passage from its position at birth by transit through the chart until it comes back to the birth degree; this is also known as a return.

Elements The four elements – earth, air, fire and water – which, along with certain other qualities, make up the signs of the zodiac. There are three signs for each element. Aries, Leo and Sagittarius are fire signs, Taurus, Virgo and Capricorn are earth signs, Gemini, Libra and Aquarius are air signs, and Cancer, Scorpio and Pisces are water signs.

Horoscope Another name for the birth chart.

House systems There are several ways of dividing up the birth chart into sectors; the systems include Placidus, Equal House, Koch and topocentric. There are no set rules as to which one should be used. Astrologers are guided by their own experience.

Houses The twelve divisions of the chart, each of which represents a different area of life.

Imum colei/IC The point at the base or nadir of the chart which represents our roots and the soil in which we grow best. It reveals factors concerning our ancestry.

Lucid dreaming This is when the dreamer becomes aware of dreaming; the dream can then be consciously manipulated.

Midheaven/MC The midheaven is the point in the chart directly opposite the IC and represents the sign and degree which were highest at the time of birth. It relates to our image in society and to our path forward in life.

NDE The near-death experience, in which people have experienced travelling out of their bodies and meeting with others who have died, or experienced communicating with beings of light. They often return to their physical form with a new perspective on life and no longer have any fear of death.

Nodes of the Moon The North and South Nodes of the Moon, also known as the Dragon's Head and Dragon's Tail, are always opposite each other. They move in a clockwise or retrograde way around the chart compared to the other planets. The North Node corresponds to the elements of the chart which we could develop and which would enhance our lives, while the South Node refers to the traits we tend to over-emphasize and which may have the effect of limiting us.

OBE An out of body experience (as in an NDE).

Opposition An aspect in which one planet or point is situated opposite another. Here, any matters concerning the planets tend to be out of balance with each other; relationships may be troublesome.

Part of Fortune This is a point on the chart which looks like a slightly compressed circle. It reveals where on the chart we have a feeling of contentment and the source of our good luck.

Personal planets Also known as the inner planets, these are Mercury, Venus, Mars, Jupiter and Saturn. Their energies are more assimilable and generally more under our conscious control than those of the transpersonal planets.

Quincunx An aspect of 150° between two planets or points. It usually denotes an area of difficulty, which, if worked on, may become an area of great strength.

Retrograde planets Where planets appear to be moving backwards, owing to the speed of the orbiting planet compared to that of the earth.

Secondary progressions More commonly known simply as progressions. This refers to a way of forecasting future trends using the number of days after birth to represent the number of years lived.

Sesquiquadrate An aspect of 135° between two planets or points; indicates a lack of ease.

Sextile An aspect of 60°, usually denoting opportunity.

Signs of the zodiac The twelve divisions of the zodiac, from Aries through to Pisces.

Square An aspect of 90°, which usually indicates a degree of conflict and tension.

Stellium A group of planets situated together in the same house or sign.

Synchronicity The phenomenon of meaningful coincidences; for example, dreaming of someone and getting a phone call from them the next day. It forms a conceptual basis for understanding such systems of divination as astrology, the I Ching and the tarot.

Transits The day-to-day movement of the planets in the sky.

Transpersonal planets The planets Uranus, Neptune and Pluto, which represent powerful energies that are outside our conscious control.

Trine An aspect of 120°, which usually denotes a measure of harmony and ease.

Zodiac An imaginary belt in the heavens which is divided into twelve equal sectors of thirty degrees, representing the constellations from Aries to Pisces.

Recommended Reading

Beginner's astrology

Hall, Judy, *The Zodiac Pack* (Findhorn Press 1996)

Hamaker-Zondag, Karen, *Planetary Symbolism in the Horoscope* (Samuel Weiser 1996)

Lawson, David, *Star Healing* (Hodder & Stoughton 1996)

Majo, Jeff, *The Planets and Human Behaviour* (Fowler 1973)

Smith, Elaine, *Astrology – The Inner Eye* (Capall Bann Publishing 1997)

More advanced astrology

Arroyo, Stephen, *Astrology, Transformation and Karma* (CRCS 1992)

Brady, Bernadette, *The Eagle and the Lark* (Samuel Weiser 1992)

Greene, Liz, *The Astrological Neptune* (Samuel Weiser 1996)

Greene, Liz *The Astrology of Fate* (Thorsons 1997)

Huber, Bruno, *Astrological Psychosynthesis* (Samuel Weiser 1996)

Idemon, Richard, *The Magic Thread* (Samuel Weiser 1996)

Psychology

Assagioli, Robert, M.D., *Psychosynthesis* (Turnstone Press 1995)

Greene, Liz and Sasportas, Howard, *The Dynamics of the Unconscious* (Arkana 1989)

Harding, Esther, M., *The I and the Not-I* (Coventure 1977)

Jung, Carl, *Selected Writings: introduced by Anthony Storr* (Fontana 1983)

Steinbrecher, Edwin C., *The Inner Guide Meditation* (Aquarian Press 1988)

Dreams

Evans C., and Newman, E., 'Dreaming: an Analogy for Computers', *New Scientist* (1964), 24, 577–9

— *Dreams and Dreaming* (Time Life Books, 1990)

Fordham, F., *An Introduction to Jung's Psychology* (Pelican Books, 1953)

Freud, Sigmund, *The Interpretation of Dreams* (George Allen & Unwin, 1961, orig. 1900)

Hearne, Dr Keith, 'Some investigations into hypnotic dreams using a new technique' (University of Reading, 1973)

— 'Visual imagery and evoked responses', (Dept. of Psychology, University of Hull, 1975)

— 'A light-switch phenomena in lucid dreams', *Journal of Mental Imagery* (1981), 5, 97–100

— *The Dream Machine: Lucid Dreams and How to Control Them* (Aquarian Press 1990

Melbourne, David, 'Dreams of Past Lives', *Horoscope* magazine, December 1996

Melbourne, David F. and Hearne, Dr Keith, *Dream Interpretation – The Secret*, (Blandford 1997)

For information about astrological dream interpretation workshops, write to David Melbourne and Helen Adams at this address:

P.O. Box 5

Lyness

Stromness

Orkney

KW16 3NN

Index